THE THAMES
FROM RICHMOND TO
PUTNEY BRIDGE
The Walker's Guide

D0994397

ENDPAPERS

Maps by John Rocque, land surveyor and cartographer (c.1704-1762).

John Rocque arrived in England from Geneva probably as a child in c.1709, one of a Huguenot family which had lived in Geneva after fleeing France. Rocque soon made a reputation for himself, introducing more elaborate and consistent schemes of hatching than his predecessors to distinguish principal features. Between 1734 and 1762 he prepared over 100 plans, maps and road books, including views and plans of gardens for wealthy patrons. In 1737 he embarked upon a large-scale survey of London and its environs, based upon true bearings and trigonometry to achieve accuracy and consistency, published in 24 sheets in 1746. On the whole the principal features are accurate. The same cannot always be said for the fields between, where his work was less diligent. Furthermore, the sheets of the London map do not quite match, indicating inaccuracy had crept in. Nevertheless, he set an outstanding standard for his time.

Rocque lived precariously. Mapmaking was extremely expensive and the profits uncertain. He remained an active member of the Huguenot community and died in 1762. His brother, Bartholomew, was a well-regarded horticulturalist and landscape gardener in Fulham, and is buried in All Saints' graveyard.

THE THAMES

FROM RICHMOND TO PUTNEY BRIDGE

The Walker's Guide

David McDowall

*with sketch maps & line drawings
by Angela Kidner*

COVER: *Boat Race*, Charles Sharland, 1913.
© TfL Reproduced courtesy of London's Transport Museum

First published by David McDowall
31 Cambrian Road, Richmond, Surrey TW10 6JQ
www.davidmcdowall.com

© David McDowall 2005

The right of David McDowall to be identified as the author of this work has been
asserted by him in accordance with the Copyright, Design and Patents Act 1988

British Library Cataloguing in Publication Data
A catalogue record for this book is available from the British Library

ISBN 0 9527847 3 4

Designed and typeset in Monotype Octavian and Formata by Peter Moore
Printed in Hong Kong

Contents

Maps

Illustrations

Figures

Acknowledgements

THE ILLUSTRATIONS

The illustrations have been reproduced by kind permission of
the Ashmoleum Museum, pp.32,36; the Barnes and Mortlake
Historical Society, pp.126,127; the Greyhound Inn, Kew Green,
p.109; the London Borough of Hammersmith and Fulham Local
History Collection, pp.172,174,186,187,188,189,190; the London
Borough of Hounslow, Chiswick Local Studies Collection,
endpapers and pp.62,65,108,116,137,141,143,144,145,153,159,
163; the London Borough of Richmond upon Thames, Borough
Art Collection (Orleans House Gallery), p.25 and Local Studies
Collection, pp.22,35,81,84,89,95,97,101,102; London's Transport
Museum, cover; Mr Patrick Loobey, pp.113,117,125,162,168,191,
203; The Museum of London, p.157; Syon Park, pp.49,55;
VosperThornycroft Group plc, p.158.

THE WORDS

A book of this kind always stands on the shoulders of previous local
studies. A basic resource has been the Historical Publications 'Past'
series with volumes covering Richmond, Kew, Brentford, Chiswick,
Hammersmith, Mortlake, Barnes and Putney. Other essential texts
have been Kim Wilkie's *Thames Landscape Strategy: Hampton to
Kew* (1994) and WS Atkins, *Thames Strategy: Kew to Chelsea* (2002).
Then there are the more detailed studies: John Cloake, *Palaces and
Parks of Richmond and Kew*, vols. I and II (1995, 1996), and his
Cottages and Common Fields of Richmond and Kew (2001); Ray
Desmond, *Kew Gardens* (1995) and John Harris, *The Palladian
Revival: Lord Burlington, His Villa and Garden at Chiswick* (1994).
There are also a number of older studies, all of which may be found
in the local studies collections of the public library service.

THE PEOPLE

One very quickly learns that while walking the ground and reading published material form the basis for a book of this kind, there are a thousand and one ways in which one is hugely dependent on the helpfulness and knowledge of other people.

First there are the staff in the local studies libraries all of whom have been extremely helpful, outstandingly Carolyn Hammond in Chiswick, Jane Baxter in Richmond and Francis Serjeant in Hammersmith. Local historians very kindly read sections of my text and caught howlers, pointed out omissions, and offered freely from their deep knowledge, notably David Blomfield, Val Bott, John Cloake and James Wisdom. Richard Pailthorpe at Syon Park and Adrian Cook at Chiswick House both gave valuable information concerning the estates for which they are responsible. Carole Ritchie took me around Kew Gardens, showing me many things that I had either not noticed or not understood. Stan Peasley regaled me about the pleasure boat business. Mark Edwards explained things from his knowledge of boats and building them. Hattie Kidner kindly read my piece on race-rowing. Peter Makower alerted me to the presence of black poplars, William Moreno supplied vital information about them, while Deborah Wolton shared her knowledge and time to join the hunt for the true native black poplar. David Wolton, her brother, shared his knowledge of brewing and read over what I had written. My son, William, told me about trees and fungi.

There are almost certainly still mistakes in the text, but for these I am entirely responsible. My grateful thanks to all the foregoing experts for their efforts to save me from worse. This is the second time Kim Wilkie has very kindly commended my work. I am particularly indebted to him.

As usual – and I am in grave danger of taking them for granted – Angela Kidner and Peter Moore both brought to this book the skills that give it real character and quality, Angela with her lovely sketch maps and figures, Peter with truly elegant and clear design. I owe a major debt to my wife, Elizabeth, who read through the text adopting the garb of an expert editor. But I dedicate the book with my love to my two sons, Angus and William, who know the river in their own way and more intensely than I ever shall.

Introduction

This second volume continues the journey started in Hampton and temporarily halted at Richmond Bridge. *The Thames from Hampton to Richmond* Bridge is frequently referred to in this current volume as vol. I, since inevitably there is plenty to refer to as one continues this unique stretch of the Thames. There is also plenty of cross-referencing, in the assumption that people will not necessarily start with Walk No 1 and work their way systematically through the book but, like myself, will be inconsistent and contrary.

In addition there are five appendices which discuss various aspects of life, on the river or along its banks. I regret that some of the content repeats what appeared in vol. I. That I am afraid is inevitable, since many people will wish to read the volume that relates to *their* stretch of the river, but not necessarily about the whole riverbank from Hampton to Fulham. Nevertheless, if you decide to read before walking, a skim through the appendices will give you a good idea of what you may wish to refer to while walking or afterwards.

As with vol. I, my purpose is to peel away the onion layers of history so that one can see what has been along the riverbank before the present, as well as what is here now. Not everything in the past was wonderful and that is certainly also true today. There have been gains and losses. Walking the riverbank one becomes increasingly aware of these. The loss of the working Thames has been a very mixed process. The decline of industrial pollution is obviously welcome, but we have lost a complex and varied river culture too. Moneyed developers can easily crowd out low-budget river activities. Newly arrived residents of the luxury *soi-disant* 'developments' carp about the noise of boat repair workshops. Do we want our river sterilised clean and dead, or mucky and muddy with human and natural activity? Do we want our river to be a beautiful, enjoyable and ecologically-inviting haven? That is a less contentious question, but can we successfully balance work, fun, beauty and ecology?

Each of us is likely to come to different conclusions about what is precious about this stretch of river. What I hope is that, despite my own ill-disguised prejudices, walkers will delight in what has gone on along the riverbank as well as much of what goes on today and forge their own criteria for safeguarding and enhancing this great river. I hope they will also be filled with sadness and anger at some of the precious things we have so casually thrown away. The river will only be properly cherished by people with passion.

David McDowall
Richmond, January 2005

WALK 1
Twickenham Park, St Margaret's, and Richmond Town

Distance 2.5 km: 1.5 hours

This is a short walk because it is dependent on the walker being able to cross the river at Richmond Lock. It explores the largely built-up suburban environment of the Middlesex and Surrey banks and what preceded it, which makes it long on words.

BEFORE YOU WALK

The Forest of Staines had once extended all the way from Staines to Brentford and the river Brent, incorporating many 'manors' or estates. This was not forest as we understand the word, for it did not imply relentless woodland but was, rather, a large tract set aside for royal hunting. Close to the river it would have been characterised by swampy areas, flood meadows, multiple river channels and small aits, or islands. By about 1230 the area was probably largely cleared of its woodland and land reclamation begun near the riverbank. Henry III gave this part of the forest, the manor of Isleworth, to his brother, Richard of Cornwall. It was an estate much larger than the present day suburb, for it included Twickenham and Whitton also.

Richard created a park on the stretch of riverbank from the present Richmond Bridge downstream possibly as far as the mouth of the river Crane known as Railshead. On the inland side it was bounded by what we now know as St Margaret's Road, which runs in an arc virtually from Richmond Bridge to Railshead, Isleworth. The park would have contained 'underwood', for fuel, implements and palings, and 'timber', standard trees, mainly oak, for the construction of houses and ships. It would also have contained livestock, cattle, sheep, deer, rabbits (in a warren) and game birds, the area probably divided internally by use of palings. It would have been bounded by a ditch and a bank with palings on top, which would soon have been enveloped in a thick hedge. All that has now gone. Had the area not been built over in the nineteenth century we should probably still be able to see these land features.

In 1415 Henry v gave part of this park as a pious foundation to the new convent of St Bridget of Syon. Across the river, facing it, he set aside another tract of land for a monastery (p. 48). He did this to fulfil the strict injunction of the Pope to his father, Henry iv. Henry iv had had his predecessor, Richard ii, foully murdered in Pontefract Castle in Yorkshire. The foundations represented a penance by the House of Lancaster for its crime against the House of York. Those familiar with *Henry v* will recall how Shakespeare imagined Henry's anxious night-time prayer before battle at Agincourt:

'Not today, O Lord!
O! Not today, think not upon the fault
My father made in compassing the crown.
I Richard's body have interr'd anew….
…. and I have built
Two chantries, where the sad and solemn priests
Sing still for Richard's soul.'

The monastery of St Bridget did not last long in the old park. The site was too wet and the best endeavours, including a massive drainage ditch, failed to solve the problem. In 1431 the nuns moved to the site of the present Syon House, which had been set aside by Henry v for the third requisite foundation, for the Celestines, a venture that remained stillborn.

After the departure of the convent the park was cleared of buildings and reverted to its previous use, primarily for livestock, until 1574 when it was granted to Edward Bacon and by 1592 was occupied by his more famous brother, Francis. Francis Bacon knew he was onto a good thing: 'One day draweth on another, and I am well pleased in my being here, for methinks solitariness collecteth the mind as shutting the eyes to sight.' It was here, probably, that he wrote his collection of *Essays*, which became an instant best-seller and remains, in the words of one eulogist: 'one of the few volumes that may be designated "world books" — books more cosmopolitan than patriotic, adapted not to an age but to all time.' So if you don't already have it, you had better buy a copy on your way home.

By now the estate was known as Twickenham Park. It so happened that the parish boundary between Twickenham and Isleworth ran slap through the house itself. When beating the bounds of the parish, a custom carried out on Rogation Sunday each year, the vicar of Twickenham or his appointee would direct a man to climb up and through a first floor window at the north-west end of the house. He then walked downstairs and joined the remaining company in the hall to sing the 100th Psalm, 'All people that on earth do dwell.' Afterwards he went back upstairs, climbed down a ladder at a window facing south-east, to continue beating the bounds. This charming madness ceased when the house was demolished in 1805 and the estate broken up and sold. From then on progressive suburbanisation took place over the whole estate. This walk, therefore, explores these developments.

Start: Proceed to the Middlesex Bank by Richmond Bridge. Take the first turning on the downstream side of the bridge, Willoughby Road.

On your left stands Caen Lodge, now known as Willoughby House, a modest Italianate delight. Built around 1840 on a plot of Twickenham Park, Caen Lodge enjoyed an open view of the river, with a paddock in front of it. It was lived in for barely a decade by the improbably named Lord Alberic Drummond Willoughby de Eresby, 22nd Baron and joint Hereditary Great Chamberlain of England. Willoughby claimed descent from the equally improbable Sir Peregrine Bertie, who swashbuckled for England in the late sixteenth century, explaining why the house was briefly called Bertie House in the 1870s.

The road you now walk along was once a path running past the paddock. It stood back from the riverbank for the then obvious reason that at high water the riverside meadows frequently flooded. In fact there was an earth bank on the landward side of the path to protect housing and pastures from flooding. The path survived until about 1880, when it was surfaced as a carriageway for newly built villas on the paddock, and was deferentially named by the locals after the man who had lived at Caen Lodge for barely a decade. On your right, Richmond Bridge Mansions were built in 1903, replacing a row of villas that had first infringed Caen Lodge's delightful aspect. In 1832 a writer extolling the beauties of the area could still say:

> '[the] footpath from the bridge at Richmond to the Isleworth [Railshead] ferry, and the greensward, here, as in Twickenham meadows, is beautiful to the very verge of the river, being still unpolluted by the towing path, which is on the other side.'

There is something touchingly innocent in finding the towpath, with its reminder of the working Thames, the 'polluting' ingredient.

Pass through the bicycle barrier at the end of the road and turn immediately left into Beresford Avenue.

The land of Beresford Avenue was still used as grazing in 1908, known as Home Farm. Josiah Clarke, dairy-farmer and local milkman, kept his herd here until his death in 1918.

It is difficult to consider any suburban development replacing open meadow so close to the Thames as anything but regressive, but one can at least enjoy this fascinating and relatively rare example of Britain's futile attempt to join the International Modern Movement. Purists would argue that *moderne* houses should have flat roofs, but here is a very British solution, with low-pitched but traditional tiled roofing, a nod in the direction of the innate deep conservatism of British suburban dwellers. But the houses have characteristically horizontal lines. The Art Deco entrances are worthy of your admiration. These *moderne* houses were about openness. You only have to look at the generous and inviting large curved windows, possibly made by Crittalls, to realise that these houses are a declaration in favour of the Outdoor Life. The Age of Sunshine has arrived, heralding the inevitable advent of sun tan lotion, wrap-around shades and the convertible sports car. Indeed, the houses were built complete with garage for a car-owning clientele, so a jar of Brylcream doubtless lurked in the bedroom.

To recognise their significance you need only proceed to the far end of Beresford Avenue, where the last few semis on the right, erected in 1935, are built in a derivative Arts & Crafts style, the last two very clearly so. They are homes that declare the attractions of indoor existence: a cosy hearth, darker rooms and with timber-framed leaded lights and vertical hanging tiles, a defence against the wintry outdoors. Which of these two styles does one pick?

On reaching Park Road at the end, turn right.

It was on this very corner that the Home Farm buildings stood. Josiah Clarke's grandson recalled:

> 'My grandfather, Josiah Clarke, moved to the farm in 1908 from 84 Hill Rise, Richmond, where he ran the milk business

from 1881, and – as a sideline– raised about 18 children [a clear testimony to what udder-warm milk can do for a chap].

His house, Park Lodge, still stands in Park Road.'

(Park Lodge, a late Regency villa, is a couple of doors back in the opposite direction.)

Opposite stands Bute Lodge, built *circa* 1828 in the late Regency Italian style, with deep eaves, a worthy companion of Caen Lodge.

Opposite Bute House stand more charming sub-Arts & Crafts houses, part of the same small development as the corner of Beresford Avenue.

Follow Park Road around to the right.

On the corner of Park Road, on your left, stands Old House Gardens, flats built in the post-1945 years of austerity.

On your right, as you proceed, stands a fine red-brick structure, the three 'Elsinore' Villas, built in 1853. Beyond them stands a graceful building, Woodlands, probably built in the 1820s or 1830s. It is unusual in that it is a back-to-back semi-detached house.

On your left stands a little gem, Victoria Cottage, another late Regency building.

When you reach the river path again, pause before turning left. Looking back along the footpath, between the path and the river stand a couple of modern private buildings. The first replaces Howlett's boatyard and chandler's shop that was still in operation in the early 1990s. The second building, Madingly Court, which stood opposite Deniel Lodge at the end of Park Road, replaces a raucous night club, the *Hooray Henry*, housed in a Victorian house that finally burnt down in 1985. It is difficult to resist the surmise that the fire was

caused by an arsonist, a sleepless neighbour of otherwise irre-
proachable probity who had finally been driven to this extremity
by its notorious late night carousing.

These apartments and the modern buildings further along result
from the shameful betrayal in 1980 of the borough's stated intention
ever since the Planning Act of 1947, to open up and protect the
riverside from Richmond Bridge to the railway bridge downstream.
One by one the open plots running down to the river have been
'developed', an oxymoron if ever there was one, for the development
of the riverbank has so often been little more than an act of
vandalism against Arcadian Thames. It is unusual to see daring
modern buildings in Richmond. If there must be buildings on the
riverfront, then *The Watermark*, designed by Edward Cullinan, is
a refreshing change from styles that take refuge in the safety of the
past.

Continue along the path, which becomes Duck's Walk.

The final victim to the pressure of developers was the boatyard
opposite the end of Riverdale Gardens. It once belonged to Charles
Lightoller, hero of the *Titanic* disaster of 1912. A plaque explains
all. Opposite the plaque is an access gate to the riverbank, from
which Richmond riverfront may be viewed.

As you proceed along Duck's Walk, note Park House Gardens on your left. This road stands on the site where the barons, in rebellion
against Henry III, supposedly encamped for almost three weeks
under their leader, Simon de Montfort, in 1263. They did so almost
certainly by permission of the landlord, Richard of Cornwall
himself (see introduction). De Montfort was the king's (and his)
brother-in-law. Richard was trying to ensure peace between the two.
It seemed for a moment as if peace indeed had been achieved. But in

March the following year rebellion broke out again, provoked it seems by Henry III's son, Edward, who staged a heist of his mother's jewels in the New Temple and pawned them to raise ready cash to pay for a royal army. It was not difficult to raise the London mob against such high-handed behaviour. The queen attempted to flee the city upstream but her boat was pelted with stones and excrement from London Bridge and she beat a hasty retreat to the more fragrant sanctuary of St Paul's. Mobs are no good when it comes to political complexity. Forgetting Richard's endeavours to bring about reconciliation, this particular mob simply recalled he was a brother of the king. So it marched on Isleworth manor, 'set it on fire, and destroied the water milles and other commodities which he there had. This deed was the cause (as some have judged) of the war that ensued.' Till then Richard was 'continuallie an entreater for peace,' but 'he was now ever after this time an utter enemie unto the barons, and unto their side, so far as laid in his power.' The rest, as they say, is history. De Montfort won a resounding victory at Lewes in May 1264, but the following year he and his army were destroyed at Evesham.

The road itself is named after Twickenham Park House, built in the 1820s. It stood about halfway down the present road. Like Orleans House upstream it fell victim to a gravel company, which excavated most of the site before the house itself was demolished. Unlike Orleans House, it was hardly an architectural gem. A major land reclamation exercise was necessary before Park House Gardens could be built.

The houses are again *moderne*, the first on the left actually fulfilling the ultimate requirement of a flat roof. Others have green tiled roofs, another tell-tale but short-lived 1930s style. If you are remotely interested in suburban housing styles, these houses too are worth a look. A few still retain their original windows.

Twickenham Park House in 1929, marooned by gravel extraction around it and demolished shortly after. Twickenham road bridge was built four years later, just to the right of the rail bridge.

Proceed along Duck's Walk.

Look out on your left for the 'The Elms', a large and imposing Victorian mansion built c.1855. The land was part of St Margaret's estate downstream and the house was constructed because the adjacent railway line cut the land off from the rest of the estate. The house stands just behind the old river flood dyke, still visible. Originally a 'Gentleman's Residence' it went down in the world to take 'City Gents as Paying Guests.' The garden is probably not greatly changed.

The railway bridge was constructed in 1848, a year after the proposal to lay the Windsor-Staines & South Western Railway was approved by Parliament. The original structure, composed of three 100-foot spans, was designed by Joseph Locke. Locke had worked with George Stephenson to construct the railway between Manchester and Liverpool in 1830, which (*pace* Stockton to Darlington (1823)) really opened the railway era. However, while the piers are his, the superstructure was entirely renewed in 1908, effectively providing two separate sets of steel arches, each carrying one track. In designing the piers Locke met the specification that they should have rounded cutwaters, appropriate for a river, with stone dressings.

Fritz Otto, a Dutch barge, has been moored beneath the bridge for at least 25 years.

Just beyond the rail bridge on your left stands a Water Board kiosk containing steps down to an inspection tunnel running under the river (to a similar kiosk on the Surrey bank).

The road bridge, thrown across the river in 1933 as part of the Great Chertsey Road scheme, is a very much more elegant piece of work than the rail bridge. The architect was Maxwell Ayrton, who had already made his name with the design of the Wembley Stadium ten years earlier. Ayrton's first plan caused apoplexy in leafy Surrey, for it proposed a pair of massive square concrete towers, 70 feet high, on the principal pier on each riverbank: 'a dramatic and fortified appearance entirely out of keeping with the surroundings' expostulated *The Richmond and Twickenham Times*. So the towers were dropped in favour of a less obtrusive structure. The engineer was Alfred Dryland, also responsible for the Great West and North Circular roads and Western Avenue.

This is the first large ferro-concrete bridge to be constructed in Britain with permanent hinges for self-adjustment. This innovation and the vertical expansion joints are emphasised by their decorative bronze plates. The arches ride on bitumen-coated compressed cork. The concrete surfaces are 'bush-hammered' to expose the aggregate in the concrete mix. The road ramps and land piers are enhanced with red tile courses, a feature characteristic of the buildings of Byzantium. The metal work is a treat: enormous bronze plates for the hinges and expansion joints, elegant balustrades, bronze lamps set into the piers and on top of the bridge itself. The latter are marred by the grossly discordant modern street lighting subsequently imposed without thought for aesthetic impact on the bridge. What, for goodness sake, is safety compared with Art? Niches were designed over the piers for sculptures but there was insufficient money for these. The bridge is sadly neglected. Every year yet another piece of crafted bronze is stolen. If you think the bronze work would look better buffed up, as it looked originally, beware. You risk ambush by a local patina-protection lobby. But some things one cannot protect. The bridge sounded the death knell for a ferry operating here since 1804.

Turn immediately left along The Avenue after the bridge.

Note the hump in the road, again part of the old flood dyke. The Avenue was the outer edge of the St Margaret's Estate, the houses and gardens on your left having been demolished for the road bridge. The estate had been acquired by The Conservative Land Society in 1854. This society, formed a couple of years earlier, had a political agenda. It was committed to the right of male householders to vote, but also to the expectation that such householders should vote Tory. The plots for sale were sized large enough to qualify owners to vote under the Reform Act of 1832.

The name 'St Margaret's' was given to this part of Twickenham Park by Archibald Kennedy, the Earl of Cassilis, after he had acquired it in about 1820. Cassilis was the ancient Kennedy strong-hold in Ayrshire. Archibald was later re-styled the Marquis of Ailsa, hence Ailsa Road nearby. Ailsa Craig is a volcanic plug that

The Conservative Land Society's vision for St Margaret's, 1854. St Margaret's House stands at the bottom of the view.

dramatically emerges from the waves off the Ayrshire coast: great for gannets, less obviously great for a marquis. As for St Margaret of Scotland, she was in fact English. Her brother, Edgar Atheling, was the royal pretender after Harold's death at Hastings.

Turn right into St Peter's Road.

This road boasts the cream of Victorian suburban villas. Some houses are so exclusive they do not even have numbers. Some of the developers acquired double plots, since size mattered so much. First, on your right stands one of the very first villas to be built: Cassilis House, named after the late departed Marquis. Fire destroyed most of the house at the end of the nineteenth century, and only the cottage and billiard room, large enough in themselves, survive now with added extensions.

On your left is a row of villas, numbers 27-21, boasting fine Victorian decorative brickwork, modestly sized by St Peter's Road standards, but generous by any others. Shame about the garages.

On your right look out for No 12. The porch looks like a cleverly added feature, given humour by its terracotta cockerel. No. 6, 'Thamesview', boasts a decorative balustrade on its roof. If one ignores the garage addition, No. 4 is an elegant Victorian mansion, with handsome bargeboards for the porch and roof.

On your right the last house, Ormonde Lodge, is egregiously large, rightly so since it was built with money won on a racehorse. It is now divided into two (still enormous) dwellings. Just beyond lies the end of the St Margaret's Pleasure Gardens. The largest part of these gardens lies behind the houses on the left side of St Peter's Road, now totally hidden from prying eyes. There is a serpentine lake, which may have been sculpted from the drainage ditch first dug for the Brigittine Monastery in the fifteenth century. If you look immediately over the wall on your right, just beyond Ormonde Lodge you may notice a slight depression very close to the house, probably the last vestige of that medieval drainage ditch.

Turn right out of St Peter's Road, cross St Margaret's Drive and go through the alley opposite.

You will know you are on the right track as a handsome holm oak partly obstructs the alley. Holm oaks were introduced from southern Europe in about 1500 (see p.200).

Turn left along the river footpath towards Railshead.

Behind the present wall on your left stood three great houses, St Margaret's, Lacy House and Gordon House, of which only the last survives. First, St Margaret's House. It was built and then rebuilt twice in less than half a century. The final version was built in 1852 by 'Black Jack' Needham, Lord Kilmorey. Kilmorey, however, actually lived in Gordon House. He had had a colourful past. He had run away from Eton to enlist and fight in the Peninsular War and had once escaped from a debtor's prison, concealed in a coffin. Already a married man, Kilmorey had been left guardian to six children when a friend died in about 1840. Kilmorey fell in love with his youngest charge, Priscilla, and they eloped. They remained deeply in love. It was almost certainly for her that Kilmorey had St Margaret's House rebuilt, but during construction she fell mortally ill, so he never lived in it. After its completion it was let to the Royal Naval Female School. It was destroyed by a bomb in 1940.

A few yards downstream stood Lacy House, built c.1750 by James Lacy, a co-manager with David Garrick of the Drury Lane Theatre. James' son, Willoughby, spent his father's substance on riotous living, entertaining local theatrical friends like the Sheridans, from Richmond Hill. One gets the picture from a guest's description:

> 'Our orgies lasted until day (with the exception of a few of the more sober guests, who departed earlier), when, about five o'clock our party of *bon vivants* sallied forth to the garden, it being a bright summer morning. Sheridan and I had a fencing match; and Jerry Orpin, brother of Mrs Lacey for a wager jumped from the lawn, his clothes on, into the stream, and swam backwards and forwards across the Thames.'

Willoughby sold his share in the theatre to Sheridan, probably because the former needed ready cash to service his lifestyle. Lacy House was later lived in by Sir Edward Walpole, elder brother of the more famous Horace. The contrast could hardly have been greater for, in Horace's words, Edward 'being very shy lived a retired life, and for several of his latter years scarcely stirred from the house....' The house was demolished in the 1820s.

The last house on this riverbank, the only one still standing, is Gordon House, previously known as 'Thisleworth' (i.e. Isleworth) and 'Railshead'. Its most important resident, perhaps, was Moses

Hart, an immigrant from Breslau who became a successful city stockbroker. He lived in the house for almost 40 years, from 1718 until his death in 1756. Hart lived in the original central section, architect unknown. Moses' brother, Aaron, was Chief Rabbi of the Ashkenazi community. Moses funded the rebuilding of the Great Synagogue in Duke's Place, Aldgate in 1721. It is nice to know that while some local people were pretty sniffy about immigrant Jews, Moses Hart and his son-in-law Aaron Franks, would assemble 'at a local clergyman's house to play cards.'

Two years after Hart's death the next owner commissioned the young Robert Adam to add a wing on the upstream side of the central building. It was Adam's very first commission in England. The upper parts of the Adam wing and the top of the central structure can been seen above the wall from the footpath.

The house acquired its name from a later resident, Frederick Gordon, son of George (Marquis of Huntly). Frederick was greatly disliked by his neighbours next door, Lord and Lady Ailsa, because in 1836 he had married their recently widowed daughter-in-law, Augusta FitzClarence (daughter of the Duke of Clarence and Dora Jordan, see vol. I, p.55) and moved into what had once been Lord Ailsa's property. Augusta's granddaughter recalled:

> 'Railshead became the scene of squabblings and family bickerings between her [Augusta] and the old Lord and Lady next door; in fact things became so unpleasant... to go on living at Railshead, next to indignant Lady Ailsa, was an impossibility...'

Augusta got daddy, now William IV, to give her a nice apartment in Kensington Palace.

Kilmorey added the clocktower and other bits of top hamper. The neo-Egyptian mausoleum close to the junction of St Margaret's Road and Drive was built for his beloved Priscilla, and houses them both.

There is no point in walking beyond the moored river craft. You have been brought this far simply for the view.

Just beyond the moored boats, but not visible from the bank, is 'Rails Head' itself, where the river Crane debouches into the Thames. The name almost certainly refers to the stakes running out from the bank, which formed the framework of a medieval fishing weir. In the late eighteenth century there was a plan to cut a canal from Railshead to Monkey Island, about 20 miles upstream of Windsor on the Thames. The canal would presumably have followed a direct route very slightly south of the M4, cutting off the major loop of the river southwards to Chertsey. It never happened.

Retrace your footsteps but cleave to the riverbank footpath and take the steps up and over the Richmond Lock.

Old London Bridge had always acted not only as a bridge but also as a weir, significantly reducing the impact of the tidal flow in both directions. With its demolition in 1832, the tidal effect was felt much more strongly as far upstream as Teddington. Its prime effect was to reduce the river between Richmond and Teddington Lock to a pathetic stream in the bed of the river at low water. The new suburban classes objected strongly to the resultant pong, doubtless caused by their raw sewage being pumped into the Thames. Meanwhile, watermen found that their vessels, even small wherries, would often run aground. It took until 1890 before Parliament approved the building of a lock and weir. The lock, completed in 1894, is in effect a 'half-lock', since its purpose is only to hold back enough of the river at low water in order to keep the upstream section reasonably full. The weir barriers are therefore raised to temper the river level. In the meantime, in this golden age of municipal achievement, sewage was dealt with by new-fangled processing plants.

Turn right to walk upstream along the Surrey riverbank.

The Old Deer Park, the land on your left, will be discussed in Walk No. 2. But you have a second chance to admire Maxwell Ayrton's road bridge with its beautiful bronze work, and to enjoy the cluster of houseboats moored on the far bank.

Just after the railway bridge resist the temptation to continue walking along the riverbank. Pause in front of the first house on your left.

This elegant house was built for Charles Asgill by his good friend, Robert Taylor. Both were self-made men. Asgill rose to be Lord Mayor of London. Taylor, son of a stonemason, rose to be one of the principal architects of his day. Both were knighted for their endeavours. Taylor died having caught a chill at Asgill's funeral.

The house, built in the early 1760s, was enlarged in the nineteenth century but fortunately restored to its original shape in 1970. The ground floor and first floor both have large octagonal rooms facing onto the river. Unusually, the ground floor was used for entertaining. One can see why. In summer Asgill's guests would naturally spill out into the garden to enjoy the Arcadian setting.

Before proceeding up Old Palace Lane, the road on the left side of Asgill House, you may care to take a seat (one is thoughtfully provided) to read a brief introduction to the royal associations with Shene/Richmond.

Before 1500, Richmond was known as Shene. Shene was a manorial estate which had reverted to royal hands in the early fourteenth century. In the mid-fourteenth century Edward III began to develop what was probably already a moated manor house as a royal palace, on a large plot of land immediately upstream from where you are seated. Edward was succeeded in 1377 by his grandson, Richard II. In 1383, aged 16, Richard married Anne of Bohemia, a political alliance that for these two teenagers rapidly became a romance. Shene became their love nest, in particular the pavilion they had built on a large ait just offshore from the palace. The pavilion was probably a standard timber-frame building on stone footings. As for the ait, it is impossible now to envisage it. Only three of several aits are left, their size almost certainly greatly reduced and changed as a result of erosion. Anne died very young, in 1394. Without Anne, Shene became an empty shell and, in his desolation, Richard had all its buildings dismantled the following year.

As mentioned in the introduction, Henry V had established a religious foundation on each riverbank; the Brigittine monastery and, on what we now know as the Old Deer Park, the Charterhouse of Shene (see p.48). He started work on a more elaborate palace and clearly had intentions to develop the whole estate but his early death in 1422 foreclosed this. Nevertheless, in due course the land all the way to Kew became associated with successive royal households.

During the minority of his son, Henry VI, the rebuilding of the palace of Shene was completed in the latest style: a semi-fortified *donjon*. It had a moat and battlements, but on the other hand it boasted large windows, an indication no serious attack was anticipated. It was this palace that Henry VII adapted and renamed 'Richmond' in 1500. By then, however, a fire had caused major damage. It is unclear how much had to be replaced, but it seems that while enlarging the palace, the central feature, in the Tudor period known as the privy lodgings, remained largely the same at least in plan. Henry renamed his palace after his erstwhile title, Earl of Richmond. Henry may have had in mind the value of a palace close to London (for it was little more than two hours away on the tide) but also far enough away to be safe from disorder or rebellion in the city,

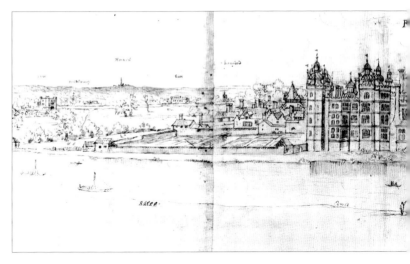

Richmond Palace, seen from the river, by Anthony Wyngaerde, 1561.
(Ashmolean Museum)

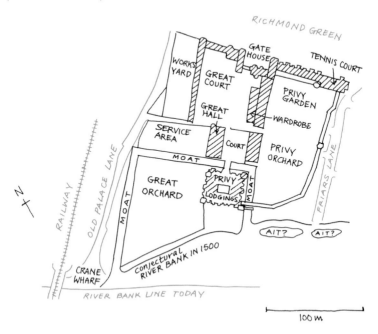

a sudden *coup de main* was something a monarch always had to keep in mind.

The layout of the palace says much about the change in kingship too. The monarch was no longer simply *primus inter pares* as his predecessors had been. The old aristocracy had been decimated in the recent wars. Henry was able to establish a greater distance between the few remaining magnates and himself. His *confidants* were no longer powerful warlords but men of proven ability and loyalty, no matter how humble their origins. His power was also more absolute. A century earlier the king was constantly surrounded by his courtiers. He probably would not even have evacuated his bowels in privacy. During the fifteenth century the idea of royal privacy had been very slowly developing. Individual privacy was an idea which slowly filtered down through society during the following centuries. At Richmond Palace one is immediately struck by the new nomenclature: Privy Lodgings, Privy Gardens, Privy Orchard, all separate from the Great Hall and Chapel. By 1500 the sovereign and his consort had withdrawn from constant public gaze. The palace may have gone, but everything we know about it announces this moment of transition.

Proceed up Old Palace Lane.

This lane ran along the side of the palace wall and moat, acting as its 'service road'. Crane wharf was where all the river-borne supplies for the palace were unloaded. The lane must have existed by the early fifteenth century but is possibly older.

On your left. In the fifteenth century this was still an open parcel of land where Henry VI created the relatively small 'New Park of Shene' in the 1430s, the nucleus from which James I created his much larger deer park in 1604 (see p.45). What one now sees, however, are the public house, the *White Swan* (originally the *Asgill Arms*) and artisan cottages (Nos. 25-14) all dating from the mid-nineteenth century. These cottages were occupied principally by men in the building trade, but also by an upholsterer, a yeast manufacturer and a straw bonnet maker. The houses have gone seriously up-market since then. Opposite, Old Palace Yard marks the old service entrance to the palace. A little further on your left are six larger houses (Nos. 13-8) built in the 1840s.

Pause when you emerge onto the Green.

The Green is what is left of the medieval area of 'common waste', where manorial tenants would have been allowed to graze their livestock. Encroached upon from the mid-fifteenth century, it has survived intact since the beginning of the eighteenth century. Even in the early years of the eighteenth century it was still used for grazing livestock and so fenced for the purpose, a nice antidote to Richmond's growing attraction to polite society for whom, however, seats were placed beneath the avenue of trees. But polite society could also be uncouth. It was the gentry that arranged for and attended the bull-baiting and prize fights on the Green.

Theatre Royal, Richmond Green.

Squeezed between Garrick Close on your right and the house on the corner of Old Palace Lane and the Green, once stood the Theatre Royal, facing along this side of the Green. The theatre flourished in its association with famous actors, among them Dora Jordan, Sarah Siddons (immortalised by Gainsborough) and the legendary Edmund Kean, who managed the theatre from 1831 till his death in 1833. It was demolished in 1884.

Turn right.

Following the piecemeal demolition of the palace from the Commonwealth period onwards, Richmond once again became a fashionable resort in the eighteenth century.

Immediately on your right stand two originally identical buildings, Wentworth House and the Old Court House, built in 1707-8. Wentworth House was substantially remodelled following severe gale damage in the 1850s. The doorway and bow of the Old Court House are late eighteenth century additions.

Continue to the gatehouse of the palace.

Both the main and postern gateways survive. Note the hinges which once supported the wooden gates. Over the gate are the (restored) arms of Henry VII.

Richmond Palace, seen from the Green, by Anthony Wyngaerde, 1561. The land approach to the palace is far less grand than from the river. (Ashmolean Museum)

Proceed into the Palace courtyard.

This is the remains of the outer, or Great, Court of the palace. On your left is the palace wardrobe, used for housing the clothing and soft furnishings of the palace. Look out for the telltale brickwork between the ground and first floor windows indicating now bricked-up carriage access. This access was almost certainly for undercover loading and unloading of the royal fabrics. Despite much later repair work, the original Tudor diaper pattern of deep purple can still be seen in the brickwork.

Straight ahead stands the Trumpeter's House, built in 1703 on the site of the Middle Gate and named after two trumpeter figures, which once decorated either side of that gate. The service area, the kitchens and outhouses for food, fuel and so forth, lay on your right, now occupied by a 1950s pastiche, the 'Trumpeter's Inn'. The riverfront of the palace features in Walk No. 2.

Retrace your footsteps to the Green and turn right.

On your right stands the 'Maids of Honour Row', a terrace of four houses built in 1725, first built as accommodation for the ladies-in-waiting of Princess Caroline at Richmond Lodge, a mile downstream (see p.76). All were in private hands twelve years later. The first of these, No. 4, boasts rooms painted by Antonio Jolli in 1745 for the resident, John James Heigdegger, manager of the King's Theatre, Haymarket and George II's Master of the Revels. Moses Hart's daughter Judith lived here from 1754-1802. Widowed early, Judith Levi entertained lavishly and distributed much of her wealth charitably, including bearing the cost of extensive refurbishment of the Great Synagogue her father had originally paid for. She enjoyed the local epithet 'Queen of Richmond Green.'

Tudor Place, after Maids of Honour Row, in origin mid-seventeenth century, was built on the royal tennis court. Enlarged in the nineteenth century, it was later converted into three dwellings.

Follow the road slightly angled to the right, past Friars' Lane on your right.

The name Friars' Lane refers to the Observant Friars (Franciscan Grey Friars), for whom Henry VII provided a home in some old timber framed buildings that stood between here and the river. The friars were driven out in 1534 when they courageously refused to acknowledge the legitimacy of Henry VIII's divorce from Catherine of Aragon and subsequent marriage to Anne Boleyn.

Just past Friars' Lane on your right: Old Friars was built in 1687 with a frontage c.1700; the next house, Old Palace Place, c.1690, bears traces that it was originally three houses and, beyond it, Oak House probably dates from the middle years of the eighteenth century.

Before entering King Street: On your left is Old Palace Terrace, composed of seven dwellings, built in 1692.

Walk up King Street.

King Street probably existed as a lane from the establishment of the palace and was certainly here by the end of the fifteenth century. But like much of Richmond town it was not paved until the beginning of the nineteenth century, so one can imagine the degree of mud and filth generated in wet weather. Look out on your right for No. 8, with its early nineteenth century print shop window and Nos. 12-14, which were built in the late seventeenth century.

On your left, the name Paved Court declares the rarity of paving at this time, c.1690. At the end of King Street you may care to refresh yourself at the *Old Ship*, a building which has been a pub since the 1680s.

Take the first turning to the right, Water Lane.

Water Lane follows the course of an old streambed down to the river. It may seem wholly unprepossessing, but this was the principal route for river-borne goods to come ashore. Enjoy the cobbles, or setts, and twin-track paving of the carriageway. The cobbles are set at an angle to allow the ponies traction when hauling loads up the hill from the river, while the paved tracks minimise friction for carts.

On your right the *Waterman's Arms* is a handsome Victorian pub but it is not the original pub of that name. The *White Cross* at the bottom of the lane was originally called the *Waterman's Arms*, in the 1720s and '30s. Before it was rebuilt in the 1830s, it was doubtless where the halers who towed barges up and down the river spent their hard earned cash, tumbling out to do service again when they heard the cry 'Man to horse!' (actually, 'Man to hawse', see p.230). Both pubs, however, still provide food nourishing enough to haul a barge. On your left, the *Slug and Lettuce* is an old brewery building. The Collins Brewery started business here in the 1720s and operated despite vociferous local opposition to the 'smoke, filth and stench' it caused until it was purchased in the 1870s to house Richmond's own waterworks. Finally, running into the river is the old drawdock. It is probably constructed on the reclamation of what was once an ait at the foot of Water Lane, used in the seventeenth century as a wharf. One may imagine much of the riverbank here once to have been swampy, with reed beds.

Turn left and look out across the river.

Near the far bank is Corporation Island, so named to mark Richmond's new borough status in 1890. Four hundred years ago it was simply 'the Bullrush bed near the Ferry Place.' Downstream are a couple of small aits, just possibly the residue of the ait on

which Richard II had his amorous retreat, but it is impossible to know for sure.

You will pass on your left Richmond's major Riverside development.

This development was designed by the classical revivalist, Quinlan Terry. 'If you understand the simplicity of Classicism,' he once remarked with evangelical fervour, 'you can apply it anywhere; it is *the* way to build; it is certainly the *natural* way to build.' The development incorporates a few genuinely old facades into a 1980s stage-set. These older buildings are Tower House (1856), Heron House (1693) and the Old Town Hall (1893) stepped back from the frontage and so not visible in the sketch.

Throughout the summer its promenades throng but not everyone is happy. The principal complaint is its intrinsic dishonesty. The *faux* Palladian and Baroque exteriors hide standard offices with low ceilings and raised floors unrelated to the proportions of the exterior. The baroque cupolas hide air-conditioning vents. The other complaint is that the development could and should have essayed the finest architecture of the late twentieth century. Debate, on your way home.

Just by the bridge, note the boathouses. They and the people who have used them feature at the outset of Walk No. 2.

Finally, the bridge (see vol. I, p.212). A ferry had operated at the site of the present bridge for several hundred years. The construction of a wooden bridge at Kew in 1759 stimulated similar thinking in Richmond. Not one to rush his fences, the ferryman finally proposed a wooden bridge in 1772. The Parish turned down his proposal because many people wanted a bridge to be sited at the foot of Water Lane. The reasons were simple. The hill behind the ferry was steep, and Water Lane gave direct access onto Richmond's main street. However, the landowner on the Twickenham shore refused point blank to allow a new thoroughfare to be cut through her estate. Thanks to her the bridge was built where the ferryman had proposed, but in stone. Funds were raised through a tontine (described in vol. I, p.212), the first stone laid in 1774 and completed in 1777.

From Richmond to Kew Bridge and back via Brentford and Isleworth

Distance 9 km: 3 hours (to Kew Bridge only, half this length/time)

BEFORE YOU WALK

This walk takes you along the towpath from Richmond to Kew. Those made of sterner stuff will choose to brave the traffic and cross Kew Bridge to walk back through Brentford and Isleworth. The softer option is to take the No. 65 or 391 bus back to Richmond from Kew Green. If you walk across the Green, there is a bus stop enticingly close to the Maids of Honour teahouse on the road to Richmond. Because you may be seduced by this prospect of tea, much of the description of the Middlesex bank is given on the walk along the Surrey bank (but do not be put off doing the whole walk, for there is plenty more on the Middlesex bank for those willing to demonstrate their mettle). Whether or not you opt for the longer walk, it will probably repay to skim through the whole walk before setting out.

Start at the foot of the steps of Richmond Bridge on the Surrey bank (downstream side).

Most of the Richmond riverfront has been described at the end of Walk No. 1. On your immediate right, however, at the foot of the steps, are boathouses built c.1850. These retreat under the terrace and seem to predate construction of the Italianate Tower House behind (1856). (See p.40 for the Riverside development). Boat-houses were almost invariably made of wood. Here, however, are boathouses of much greater usefulness, for the damp cool conditions created by the brickwork are perfect for the storage of boats.

Richmond was already well established as a playground for the gentry in the second half of the eighteenth century. William Hickey was one of these *bons viveurs*. Writing in 1781, he recorded in his journal:

> 'In July I hired one of Robert's eight-oared barges and a smaller boat to attend with horns and clarionets, having previously invited a party to dine with me at the Castle at Richmond [the leading hotel, situated on Hill Street]....
> The plan we had arranged was, having dined, &c., to take wine on board our boat and row gently down to Vauxhall and there sup.'

The heyday for Richmond's watermen proved to be the 70 years or so up to the Second World War. It came as an unexpected reprieve following the advent of good carriageable roads, river steamers and, above all, the railway, which had rapidly destroyed the traditional river economy. Watermen now hired out pleasure skiffs to the burgeoning middle classes. In the mid-1930s there were about 4,000 pleasure boats licensed with the Port of London Authority just for the half-tidal Thames, that is between Richmond and Teddington locks. By then horns and clarinets had given way to wind-up gramophones and jazz. (If you are interested to know more about the pleasure boat trade and its decline, see p. 235.)

Continue your walk past the Riverside (p.40).

Straight after the terrace, the ground level doors facing the river are former boathouses, possibly dating back to the 1830s.

Pass the bottom of Water Lane.

Just beyond the *White Cross* pub stands St Helena Terrace, built in
the mid-1830s for prosperous members of the middle classes, who it
was expected would commute into London. By 1830 there were five
omnibuses a day to Bank and another to St Paul's. By 1843 six river
steamers ran in each direction, daily, rather more delightful than
strap-hanging on the District Line. The boathouses below, built at
the same time, replaced boathouses, probably of timber, used not
only for boats but to accommodate merchandise, very probably coal
and possibly the carts used to convey the coal and other merchandise
to and from local destinations. Lighters carrying coal came up from
the Port of London regularly. Several lightermen and boatbuilders,
some of whom lived in Water Lane, owned or rented the sheds. One
may picture the scene here, with a large amount of traffic all around
the old drawdock at the end of Water Lane. Anxious to catch the tide
to continue their journey, be it the flood to go upstream or the ebb
downstream and with a queue of other barges anxious to offload
and do the same, time was of the essence for lighters and barges
(see p.228). One would have seen feverish off- and on-loading, with
merchandise waiting on the quayside to go onto barges and other
merchandise having just come off.

Further on one passes the grounds of Richmond Palace (see p.32)

The whole of the promenade path along here is reclaimed land.
The river was wider in Tudor times, with the bank probably about
50 paces to your right. Look out on your right for the Trumpeter's
House, built 1704 with portico and wings added in the 1740s. Its
entrance stands in the grounds of Old Palace Yard (p.36).

On your left is the *Lilian*, the vessel with the ochre steam funnel.
Built in 1916, it was the largest motor yacht that had been built in

Sweden at that time.

On your right stands Asgill House (p.30).

Pass under the two bridges.

A towpath suitable for horse-drawn barges was only established along the Surrey bank from Richmond to Kew in 1777. A previous towpath had run along the Surrey bank from Kew up as far as Railshead (see p.29) where the halers (see p.228) had to cross to the Middlesex bank. The new towpath was an important improvement for the transit of waterborne goods at a time when canals also were the rage. No one moved anything heavy overland if they could possibly send it by water. With the digging of canals at this time England's transport network was transformed. There is a hint of stern efficiency in the laying of the towpath. The present path is much higher than the original towpath.

The ditch on your right seems already to have existed by this time. The channel and its banks, running to Kew, now form a vital wildlife reserve. Its vitality and significance lie in its daily tidal flushing.

Pause on emerging from under the Twickenham Bridge.

The immediate margin of ground alongside the river was, of course, almost unbroken flood meadow. But further inland the open greensward, now known as 'The Old Deer Park', is a remnant of the enclosure made by the new Scottish King, James I, on his accession to the English throne after the death of Elizabeth I in 1603. James was a dedicated huntsman. He had inherited a small triangle of land including where you now stand and, 'needing' more space in the way autocrats do, he extended it northwards across tenanted land previously belonging to the monastery founded by Henry V a couple of hundred metres lying downstream (see below). James's deer park extended well into what is now Kew Gardens but omitted the site of the actual monastery, which still had many of its old buildings, some very dilapidated, and was now tenanted. James has always had a bad press in England. Yet he had *sangfroid* fit for a king. Three days after the attempt on his life (the Gunpowder plot, 5 November 1605), and with the country in a state of acute tension, King James rode to Richmond with the intention of hunting, in defiance of his minders who counselled staying behind safe walls.

Pause on arrival, on your right, at the 'sight line' on the meridian line running from Kew Observatory.

Ignore the Crown Estate's sight line marker and its blurb. Both are (currently) mistaken and misleading. The Observatory, visible in the distance with its cupola, was designed in great haste by the architect William Chambers, at the request of George III. George was anxious to witness the transit of Venus across the face of the sun, calculated to occur on 3 June 1769. In the 1770s the observatory set the official time in London and a set of three obelisks were erected in 1778 to define two meridian lines. (A meridian line merely marks the direction of True North and True South. A meridian line may consequently be drawn anywhere, as long as it observes this requirement.) If you look a few metres to your left you will see two of the three original obelisks. The left-hand obelisk is in True North-South alignment with another obelisk on the far (northern) side of the observatory (which you will come to later). This meridian line runs through the *west* room of the Observatory. This line was used as the calibrated axis for tracking the movement of heavenly bodies by the telescope erected in the west room of the Observatory. The right hand obelisk is for a second meridian line running to the *east* room of the Observatory. It was to calibrate the alignment of a mural quadrant, used to measure the angle of a heavenly body from the earth's surface. A later and smaller obelisk on this eastern meridian is just visible near the far side of the greensward. It was erected when a much smaller transit telescope was installed in the eastern wing of the Observatory.

Kew Observatory ceased to operate as an observatory in 1840, but became the principal meteorological office, its 'k.o.' mark becoming a quality mark for meteorological instruments. Among those who worked at Kew was Francis Galton, who coined the term 'eugenics' to propagate the fell theory of improving the human species by selective parenthood. Galton, whose scientific interests were manifold, was appointed to the Observatory's management committee. He worked on a method of standardising sextants and other angular instruments using a mirror at the Observatory to flash the sun's rays onto a mirror on one of the southern obelisks. He was defeated by our usually sunless climate. The Meteorological Office left the building in 1980.

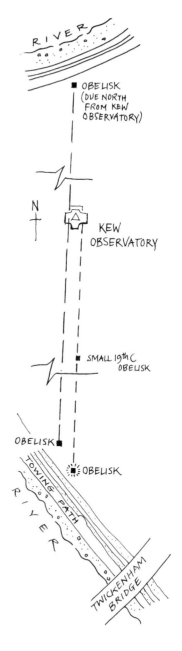

Just after Richmond Lock one gets a better view of Gordon House on the Middlesex bank (see p.27), particularly its two historic central sections. Beyond Gordon House and the cluster of moored boats the mouth of the River Crane will be seen adjacent to a drawdock. The tidal mouth of the Crane is an important spawning ground for Thames fish. In the past, however, the river was also an ideal size for water mills. A couple were sited upstream of Twickenham in the eighteenth century, one producing linseed oil and oil-cake cattle feed. Another, near Whitton, made gunpowder and this was the scene of occasional explosions, three in 1772 alone, one of which blew in Horace Walpole's antique painted windows at Strawberry Hill. The last mill closed in 1927, its remaining trace being the Crane River Shot Tower. Gunpowder mills were sited on the Crane because alder and willow growing along the riverbank made perfect charcoal, an essential ingredient of gunpowder. The land was still relatively open, so the occasional explosion inconvenienced only a few. It was a short journey downstream to the City from Isleworth quayside. Horses drawing carts of gunpowder from mill to quay would be shod with copper to avoid the danger of sparks.

On your right.

Beyond the present ditch and the trees once stood the Charterhouse of Jesus of Bethlehem of Shene, the monastery founded by Henry V in 1414 (see p.15). It interrupted the otherwise unbroken strip of flood meadow along the riverbank. The Carthusians were reclusive, each monk living in seclusion but meeting for communal worship. Unlike the gutsy Observant Friars (p.38), the monks of Shene acquiesced in Henry's break with Rome. This failed to save the foundation, which was compelled to surrender its property and the site in 1538. Thereafter, the site was converted into a private mansion and was home to the hapless teenager, Lady Jane Grey,

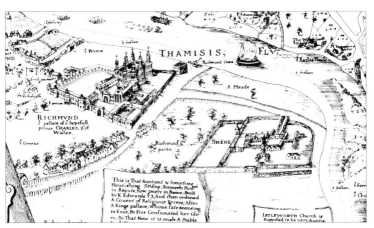

A section of Moses Glover's map, 1635, showing Richmond Palace and what remained of the Charterhouse of Shene a century after its dissolutiion.

'the Nine Days Queen' so ruthlessly beheaded by Queen Mary in 1554. The monastery enjoyed a brief reinstatement with Mary, but after her death in 1558 a number of houses progressively replaced the monastery and became known as West Sheen, harking back to the pre-Tudor place name. In due course part of the site was leased to Sir William Temple, one of the keenest gardeners of the second half of the seventeenth century. John Evelyn, the diarist, visited twice, in 1678 and again in March 1688:

> 'the most remarkable things are his orangery and gardens, where the wall-fruit trees are most exquisitely nailed and trained, far better than I ever noted.'

Daniel Defoe advised all those who read *A Tour through the Whole Island of Great Britain* that the gardens

> 'were his [Sir William's] last delight in life, so they were every way suited to be so, to a man of his sense and capacity, who knew what kind of life was best fitted to make a man's last days happy.'

So take note.

You will pass Isleworth Ait close to the Middlesex bank. Once at least six islets, it was progressively absorbed into one. In the nineteenth century the island was largely osier beds. Herons frequently stand to attention in serried rank along its bank, only right and proper for an island leased to the London Wildlife Trust.

Tucked just behind the north end of the ait lies the mouth of the Duke of Northumberland's River, originally known as Monk's River, cut from the River Crane by the Brigittine monastery after their move downstream (see p. 15) to power water mills. One of these was later used for copper, brought as ore all the way from the Mendips.

Pause opposite Isleworth.

Isleworth village today must be one of the most peaceful views on the river. Defending the parish territory, however, has not always been peaceful. Each Rogationtide (usually in May, the three days before Ascension Day) parish bounds were walked by a small party led by the vicar. At critical points, for example a tree marking a change of boundary direction, a passage from the Gospels would be read out. There was always the chance that the boundary would be disputed, as in the following parish record dated just before the Reformation:

> 'so retornyng homwarde from Babor-bryge [over the River Crane on the Staines Road, west of Hounslow] where as they said a gospell, as they had don of old tyme, peseably, and intendyng noo malyce to any person; but went along by their boundes and dyche-syde tyll they kam nyghe unto the grete hawthorn stondying in the said heth [Hounslow Heath]. Ther kam the parishe of Heston with their processyon; and, before all their banners and cross of Heston aforesayd, ther kam 5 or 6 of the parishioners of Heston, and badde one John Browne,

our foremoste bannerman, to avoyde the dyche syde; he sayd a wold not, he went upon their owne boundes. With that kam in John Bygg steppyng yn & swore an othe, "Knave, would thow not avoyde the waye, thou shallte into the dyche." With that threw hym into the dyche with his banner.'

The altercation rapidly became a general affray. Heston clearly bred big rough boys. No less a person than the vicar of Heston casually threw a young Isleworth lad and his banner into the ditch, thereby giving real meaning to the concept of muscular Christianity.

Looking from right to left, on the far right stands the domed Pavilion boathouse of Syon House. It was built in the late eighteenth century to a plan by James Wyatt (the man whose restorations irredeemably damaged several gothic cathedrals) as a surprise gift from the 2nd Duke to his wife. Whatever her reaction at the time, doubtless she later took delight in the fact that their son, the 3rd Duke, exercised by swimming to it daily from Richmond Bridge, a feat that, even on the ebb, would demolish most of us.

The church, All Saints, still boasts its fifteenth century Kentish ragstone tower. The rest, however, built in 1705, was destroyed by arson in 1943. The shell remains but a refreshingly frank but skilful modern structure, designed in 1969 by Michael Blee, has been built alongside it.

Do not be misled by the white 'gothic' house to the left of the church. It acquired its façade in 1971 to camouflage a couple of Edwardian cottages, now knocked into one.

Ferry House on the left of the gothic façade was for a while home to J.M.W. Turner, where he filled sketchbooks with river scenes. Further to the left stands *The London Apprentice*, first recorded in 1731. The drawdock in front of the row of houses was for the village. The mills and other commercial ventures had their wharves hidden from view, tucked behind the ait.

Continue downstream.

On your left, unless it is high water, there are plenty of areas of shingle you may like to explore to get an idea of the natural shore, free of embankment. A few parts of the foreshore bank are protected by 'willow-spiling', roughly woven shoots of willow which take root in the mud to form a live fence.

After 200 metres or so, look out on your right for the Northern Obelisk and behind it, the Observatory. Lying on True North from the west room of the Observatory this obelisk was 'constantly being made use of as a reference mark in determining the angle of variation of the compass needle.' The compass needle indicates magnetic north, which of course, is different from True North. If this seems confusing, the basics are: the earth spins on an axis which passes through the North and South Poles. These are True North and True South, and meridian lines must run from one pole to the other. The direction of a compass needle varies from True North because the magnetic pull of the earth's mass varies slightly from True North. Magnetic variation varies from one part of the world to another and the degree of variation is geographically and chronologically inconsistent. In Britain magnetic north is currently about 4° west of True North. Half a century ago it was 10° west of True North.

Pause when you note on your right that the ditch has become a ha-ha, with a wall beyond the ditch, almost certainly the work of 'Capability' Brown, whose work here is discussed briefly in Walk No. 3, p.99. This is approximately where a broad avenue was laid in 1695 to the river from James I's hunting lodge, a little inland in his deer park. The deer park was long neglected, first because Charles I created his much larger hunting park at the top of Richmond Hill, then because of the Civil War and Commonwealth and finally because Charles II favoured Windsor as his country retreat,

Richmond Palace being a ruin by the time of his restoration. So it was King William who, relishing the hunt, decided to improve and enlarge James' hunting lodge in 1693 and then, a couple of years later, instructed that broad formal avenues be laid, one leading to the Green in Richmond, and the other to the river bank, with an angled view of Syon House across the water. The house became known as Richmond Lodge.

Kew Gardens begins roughly when the Brentford tower blocks come into view in the distance. This part of the Gardens is left wild. Somewhere here, along this sylvan stretch, you must confront the tragedy that occurred on Monday, 15th March 1920. In the words of the *West London Press*:

> 'PC Cattell 1001 V, said he was on duty near Kew Gardens Walk, about 6 o'clock on Tuesday [16th] morning, when he saw the body of a woman lying face downwards in the backwater of the Thames. He recovered the body and summoned the Divisional Surgeon of Police, who pronounced life extinct. Witness added that he found a small bunch of chestnut buds (produced) by the waterside and an examination revealed that one of the twigs had snapped off a bough of a tree which overhung the water. The bough was out of reach and, in order to secure it, the deceased had apparently stood on two stumps of wood with the idea of pulling it down with the aid of an umbrella which was found close to the body.'

You would not have been assailed by so melancholy a tale had the victim, Edith Holden, not become a household name following the publication of her nature study artwork as *The Country Diary of an Edwardian Lady* in 1977. She was only 48 when the tragedy occurred. In her lifetime she had been a book illustrator.

Take a seat, briefly, facing Syon House on the opposite bank.

The house stands on the site of the Brigittine monastery (see p.15), begun in 1426 when the east Twickenham site seemed so damp. The monastery was suppressed in 1539. It is nice to know that generous pensions were assigned to the community. Syon was the last of the great monastic foundations to be dissolved.

Behind the ashlar (dressed stone) façade, much of the structure, including three of the corner towers, is essentially sixteenth century, with plenty of brickwork to prove it. The site had been acquired by the Lord Protector Somerset in 1547, and he set about converting the monastic buildings, or their foundations, for a mansion. It was here in 1553 that Lady Jane Grey reluctantly and fatally accepted the crown offered her by her father-in-law, John Dudley, Duke of Northumberland, and other Protestant nobles.

The battlements were added in 1609, after the freehold had been granted to Henry Percy, Earl of Northumberland in 1604. The lion on top of the building is the crest of the Percy family and came here from Northumberland House in Charing Cross when this was demolished in 1874 to make way for Northumberland Avenue. Robert Adam remodelled the interior of the house in the 1760s, a formidable task given the different ground floor levels inside the house.

Today the grounds are the legacy of Capability Brown, who apparently acquired his epithet from his habit of assuring prospective clients that their grounds possessed 'great capabilities'. William Cowper lauded him in verse:

'Lo! He comes,
The omnipotent Magician Brown appears.
He speaks; the lawn in front becomes a lake;
Woods vanish, hills subside and valleys rise;
And streams – as if created for his use –
Pursue the track of his directing wand....'

At Syon, Brown demolished the old wall surrounding the house, removed the old formal *parterres* in favour of an invisible transition

Syon House, by Jan Griffier, c. 1710, indicates the highly formalised walled gardens that preceded Brown's landscape. On the left, Ormonde (later Richmond) Lodge is far too close to the river bank, and the background gives way to a lot of fantasy. But one gets a very good idea of the terrace built by Ormonde and extended by Queen Caroline.

from lawn to flood meadow, by means of a ha-ha, a gardening technique in use by gardeners at least a generation earlier. One can just make it out, a dark shadowy line in the grass just below the house. Brown's landscaping, considerably lost through the growth of scrub during the past 80 years, is now being clawed back.

The Brigittine abbey church ran out from the present house (the church's west end) towards Brown's ha-ha. It was only completed in 1488 and demolished following the Reformation, so it existed for a comparatively short time. The foundations were only re-discovered in 2003. Size clearly mattered, for the abbey church proved to have been as large as Salisbury Cathedral, 100 metres in length and 40 metres in width. Knowing the size of the abbey church it comes as no surprise that this great foundation was, by 1500, one of the leading intellectual centres of pre-Reformation England.

This stretch of the Thames is one of its critical wetland corridors, on account of its particular ecology as tidal meadow, inundated twice daily. There is nothing downstream to compare. From the Surrey bank one can see the dominant poplar and willow tree cover, but also a transition inland from mud reed beds to flood

meadow. It is a perfect environment for marsh foxtail, meadow
sweet and flag iris, and also habitat for the rare German hairy snail,
perforatella rubiginosa to the cognoscenti. If you wonder why it is
rare and declining, it is quite simply because we have destroyed its
habitat, scruffy reed beds along the river.

Syon's reputation as a garden centre was acquired when the
house was first built by Protector Somerset. The 'father of English
botany', Dr William Turner, had a hand in the laying out of Syon
garden, where his primary roles were as Somerset's chaplain and
physician. Appropriately enough he lived in Kew, where he did
indeed have a small botanical garden. The preface to his ground-
breaking work, *Names of Herbes*, published in 1548, was written
at Syon and dedicated to his patron.

Turner was a north-countryman who definitely belonged to the
awkward squad. An early Puritan, he absented himself during
Mary's brief reign, 1553-58 and on his return took a strong dislike
to the 'Popish' garb and ritual adopted by the Anglican church. He
conceived a particular hatred for the square cap worn by bishops,
a breed for whom he had a very low regard. It was reported to the
Secretary of State who had issued the clerical dress regulations that
Turner had 'enjoined a common adulterer to do his penance in a
square priest's cap.' Worse was to come. As Dean of Wells, Turner
invited his Bishop to dinner, having carefully trained his dog
beforehand. Once the bishop was seated, in the words of a Puritan
tract, 'the dog flies at the Bishop and took off his corner-cap – he
thought belike it had been a cheesecake – and so goes the dog away
with it to his master.' Even if you are not interested in botany, here is
a one-man-and-his-dog achievement worthy of our admiration. But
the prelates were not amused and Turner was suspended from his
duties. Turner's career as priest may have ended in ruin but for the
first records of British flora, his own cap cannot be snatched.

Back to the garden. Its renown for horticulture, not simply for an idealised landscape, was restored in 1855 when it produced the first mangosteen to fruit in England. Nine years later a coconut palm was coaxed into fruit in the glass house. Only much later did Syon's gardeners realise that they could make serious money out of their horticultural skills. They have never looked back.

If you wish to consider the immediate Kew Gardens landscape behind you, turn to p.99. Otherwise continue walking.

Look out for mouth of the river Brent/Grand Union Canal on the Middlesex bank. The built-up area to its left, abutting Syon, was once an island, 'Old England', and seems to have been an important Bronze Age site. An enormous number of Bronze Age artefacts have been found in the area and in the riverbed. Was it a trading post? Was the site sacred? Brent is a corruption of the P-Celtic (the basis of Welsh/Cornish/ Breton) word meaning 'Holy Water'. So where the 'Holy Water' debouched into the 'Dark Water' ('Thames' also seems to derive from P-Celtic) may have been a sacred spot. Old England is also possibly the site of Caesar's fording of the Thames in 54BC, and an even more likely one for Claudius' crossing in 43AD.

It is also here, but on the Surrey bank, that the Anglo-Saxon Chronicle tells us that King Edmund (Ironside) defeated the Danish king, Cnut, in 1016. Edmund had already driven the Danes southwards at Tottenham but the latter had crossed by ship to the Surrey bank and started marching westwards. Edmund rushed to head them off. The battle of Brentford (more properly Kew) brought only temporary respite. The Danes rallied, then Edmund died and by the end of the year Cnut was uncontested King of England.

The Brent was probably not navigable until a channel was cut from Brentford to Braunston, near Daventry in Northamptonshire, 1793-1800. The intention was to streamline the shipment of goods that had previously travelled south-west to Oxford before travelling

south-east by the Thames to London. For almost half a century
canals became the haulage routes of Britain, until displaced by
railway. Rail came to Brentford docks in 1859. Thus Brentford
became an important *entrepôt* for the Port of London, first for the
canal system, and then for rail.

Pass the car park.

It was not meant to be like this, full of cars. George III had long
wanted to build a new palace at Kew. This is where, in 1801, James
Wyatt started work on a massive and forbidding castellated
four-storey structure. By 1811 with the roofing still unfinished,
£500,000 already spent on it (approximately £15 million today)
and the king in a state of mental collapse, the project was
abandoned. But it was also ground-breaking in its engineering.
For it was a pioneer iron-framed building, forerunner to later steel-
framed buildings. But with dry rot spreading through its woodwork,
it was decided to demolish it in 1827. So resistant did it prove to
normal demolition blandishments that it had to be blown up.

George III's castellated palace.

Look out on your left for the three aits. These were mainly osier beds until the nineteenth century. The first, Lot's Ait, acquired a barge building yard in the nineteenth century. Between the second and third aits, you will catch a glimpse of St George's church, re-designed by Arthur Blomfield in 1887, its hexagonal tower of Kentish ragstone dating from 1913. It is in danger of demolition.

This was one of the few fordable points on the river 2,000 years ago and another possible location where Caesar took his army across the river in 54BC. It is also probably approximately where Kew derived its ancient name: 'Cayho.' For there was a quay ('*cay*') somewhere on this promontory ('*ho*') contained by the encircling river. Until the eighteenth century this was still the principal ferry crossing, but this site slowly fell into disuse with the progressive enlargement of the royal gardens and the erection of Kew's first bridge half a mile downstream.

The third, downstream, island once had a tavern. The *Swan* inn opened for business in about 1724. It thrived on fashionable river traffic. In 1781 that beguiling *roué*, William Hickey, sought to *avoid* debauchery at the behest of his brother who had exhorted him:

> ' "William, ... let you and I therefore get out of the way of temptation, mount our horses and ride gently to Richmond, Brentford Ait.... where we might take a quiet dinner, a pint of port each, and jog soberly home in the evening." To so steady a plan, which I really liked, I readily consented. The event, however, never answered; entirely the reverse. The first excursion of this kind that we made we dined upon the Island off Brentford, where there is a house famous for dressing pitchcocked eels, and also for stewing the same fish. And got so completely intoxicated we were incapable of mounting our horses and obliged to take a post-chaise to convey us home. The wine being remarkably good, we ordered bottle after bottle until poor prudence was quite drowned.'

Finally, in 1812, a wealthy neighbour, Robert Hunter, whose house (now the Herbarium) on Kew Green backed onto the river, could stand it no longer. Outraged by the riotous nuisance occasioned by the carousing, he successfully acquired the island and promptly closed the *Swan*. Hunter died the same year, and one inevitably suspects that mounting blood pressure had something to do with it. At about the same time poplars were planted on the aits to protect Kew from the sight of the 'inferior buildings of Brentford.'

Just beyond the third ait rises the campanile of the Great Junction Waterworks, now the Kew Bridge Steam Museum, built in 1838. The campanile, or standpipe tower, is 60 metres high. Originally the standpipe was simply a metal structure, but it was not strong enough to take the weight and the wind, hence the 1867 brick campanile.

Keep walking until almost in the shadow of Kew Bridge. Watch out for the turning to your right at the end of the fancy spear-headed railings through Bush Road/Kew Park Estate to Kew Green. It is your moment of choice, whether to press on to explore the Middlesex bank or look at Kew Green.

While mulling over your choice, you may like to know:
It is here that in the second half of the eighteenth century Kew's two best known waterman dynasties maintained boathouses for their trade. Both became intimately connected with royalty in Kew. The Hilliers were from Brentford and settled in Kew probably in the late 1720s. William Hillier regularly took butter from Kew to St James's Palace for the royal slice of bread, be it for Prince Frederick or Princess Augusta (see p.82). He was still on their books in 1768. But the Hilliers were eclipsed by the rival family Layton. The Laytons had been operating in Kew since 1675 if not earlier. One of them, Thomas, entered the Dowager Princess Augusta's

employment in 1768, to bring exotic plants from ships docked in the City of London, and seed and seedlings from London nursery-men to her new botanic garden. He also supplied her with a lot of coal. Coal may have had less *cachet* than providing butter for the royal breakfast table, but it was almost certainly more profitable. (For more on watermen generally, see p.234.)

So, your choice at this point:
● **Succumb to the temptation of a shorter walk around part of Kew Green, refreshment at the Maids of Honour teahouse close to the bus stop for 65 or 391 bus, a little way along the Kew Road towards Richmond.**
In which case turn to ➡ page 72.

● **Or walk back to Richmond via Brentford docks and Isleworth.**
In which case, cross Kew Bridge.

The original bridge was built in 1759 by a Robert Tunstall who already operated a ferry here. A century earlier, his eponymous forebear had defied the principal ferry upstream to provide one here, partly to serve the lime kilns he owned on the Brentford bank. (You can find out more about the bridge on p.106). Lime kilns burnt chalk or limestone for the production of lime for mortar. They were often constructed at the site of building works.

Descend the steps on the Middlesex Bank. Turn upstream along the riverbank footpath. After 350m turn right (only an apartment block lies ahead), up the steps to Brentford High Street. Turn left and left again after 50 metres into Waterman's Park. Follow the riverbank terrace past the Waterman's Centre.

The Waterman's Park replaces the gasworks. The heavy concrete

Brentford as it might have been: Howard Lobb's redevelopment plan of 1944, converting the aits into a public park and replacing a swathe of old Brentford.

posts rising out of the riverbed were for mooring when unloading the coal. As for the Centre itself (built 1982-84), it replaced a large brewery. Make your own verdict on whether it fulfils the opportunity of this riverbank site. Cast an eye, too, at the re-development proposal of 1944 for Brentford High Street and the riverfront. It remained stillborn because of post-war austerity. It was the brain-child of Harold Lobb, who designed the Festival of Britain in 1951.

Lot's Ait still boasts a conglomeration of boat repair sheds, not yet tidied out of existence.

Continue around the office buildings, until you are again compelled to ascend to the High Street. Turn left and left again 100 metres later, down Goat Wharf. Follow the promenade around the docks as far as you can.

On your right you will pass an early eighteenth century building. Now heavily restored, it was the office of the Thames Soapworks

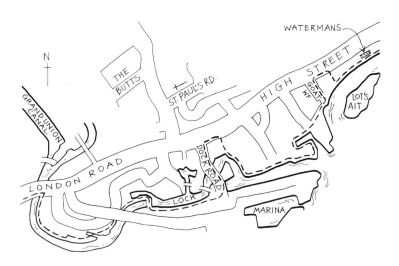

from the late eighteenth century. Soap was traditionally made from wood ash and tallow. Its manufacture was an expensive handicraft, less because of the process than because for centuries it had been taxed. In the eighteenth century soap-boiling pans were fitted with lids, locked nightly by tax collectors to prevent unmonitored production. In 1816 soap cost about one shilling per pound weight, of which one quarter, 3d, was tax. So one did not wash too often. The tax was abolished in 1853. The adjacent dock became known as Soap Creek. The business was bought by Laurence Rowe in 1799. When he died in 1824, his two bachelor sons took over. So noted were they for their good works and generosity of spirit that Dickens is said to have based the brothers Cherryble in *Nicholas Nickleby* on them. The building was later used by an engineering firm. All this newly residential area was once the engine room of Brentford's economy.

Keep walking round the dock area until compelled to return to the High Street.

A diversion for the energetic, but if you wish to skip it, go to p.66:
Across the road and the car park you will see the spire of St. Paul's
Church, where you may see the Zoffany *Last Supper* (for the
background story, see p.110) and take refreshment (on most
weekdays, recommended comestibles). Judas Iscariot, supposedly
a lawyer at St Anne's, Kew, is third from the right. Zoffany's young
wife modestly modelled for St John, appropriately resting on Jesus'
bosom, while Zoffany equally modestly depicted himself as no less
a person than St Peter. The church merits inspection because of the
skilful redesign, 1990-92, by Michael Blee, his last important work.

Having already abandoned the route of this walk, it would surely
be a dereliction of duty not to admire The Butts, arguably the best
extant group of late seventeenth and early eighteenth century
dwellings in west London.

**So, without prevarication, turn right out of St Paul's, turn right
up Half Acre and almost immediately left into the Butts.**

At the far end you will be ambushed by a delight: a small informal
market town square of late seventeenth and early eighteenth century
houses. Before entering the square, cast your eyes up the road to
the right, the Upper Butts, to the house at the end. Although the top
storey is nineteenth century, the frontage retains its charm. As you
look around the square you may be struck by the generous frontages.
Just compare them with the much more cramped contemporary
houses of, say, Queen Anne's Gate, Westminster. Land in rural
Brentford was not nearly at the same premium.

It was in front of these buildings that hustings were erected for
the county of Middlesex elections. In the eighteenth century the
elections here often ended in affrays. In 1768, when the controversial
but celebrated John Wilkes was elected Member for Middlesex,
one man was killed, and in the election the following year another

fatality occurred here. The peaceful character of the Butts had been violated before. Prince Rupert's cavalry came this way in 1642, and doubtless sacked the houses that were standing here (see below). A century earlier it was a scene of the Marian persecution. In July 1558, Six Protestants put on trial in London had been condemned for refusing to recant. Brought to Brentford after dark, they were burnt the next day. Long before the religious conflicts of the Reformation, the Butts acquired its name from the archery practice required of able-bodied men on manorial estates the length and breadth of the realm. Agincourt, one might say, was won in the butts.

In the lowest corner of the square stands the now privately owned Boatmen's Institute, a recent interloper, backing onto the canal and replacing Brentford's mill. It was built in 1904 by the London City Mission to provide schooling for

The watermill that made way for the Boatmen's Institute, demolished 1904.

boat children while the older members of their families attended to the loading or unloading of their narrow boats. It was a formidable challenge. As a report in 1906 observed:

> 'No two days have we the same children and rarely if ever have we the same children in morning and afternoon. While some will be back again shortly, with others it may be months. Yet with these drawbacks it is remarkable how well many of them are getting on. Some of those who are beginning to read are lent books to help them while they are on their journeys...'

Thus, by human agency, miracles can indeed happen.

Retrace your steps to Half Acre, almost opposite St Paul's. Turn right, back down to the High Street. Cross the High Street at the traffic lights, turn left and right almost immediately into Dock Road.

Coming from the High Street (top of p.64) turn left and after 75 metres turn left into Dock Road.

Brentford Dock was built in 1855 when the Great Western Railway acquired the Brent's delta. GWR needed a railhead for goods bound for export to the New World via Bristol, and to a lesser extent, goods coming from the West Country, bound for the Port of London. Brunel had already acted as Chief Engineer to the GWR since 1832. Now he created the masterplan for the new dock and improved waterways. Brentford Dock was opened the year of his death, 1859. It closed in 1964 when Beeching was axing the railways.

Cross the two dock bridges.

These bridges were built in 1859 to accommodate a broad gauge railway laid from Southall to Brentford Dock, for the carriage of goods. The track became obsolete in 1876 when a standard gauge line was laid a little further west.

Turn immediately right, down the steps and along the Brent canal footpath. After 200 metres you will have to turn left up steps and double back to your right across the footbridge over the canal.

This area suffered massive inundation in the dramatic flash flood of January 1841. Throughout the previous December the weather had been colder than any December for at least 40 years. The ground was deeply frozen. Between the 10th and 15th January there was extremely heavy precipitation: both rain and snow. On the 16th a

Brentford Lock, c. 1905, looking towards St Lawrence's Church on the High Street, closed but still standing in 2004. The Ham lies to the left (west) of St Lawrence's.

thaw set in and by midnight people started to notice the water level rising in the canal but no one thought anything of it. As the *Times* reported:

> 'Towards 2 o'clock, however, Police-constable Smith T60, who was on duty near the bridge [which you will shortly reach], observing the water still increasing and rushing with great force to the Thames, awakened some of the boatmen belonging to what are called "monkey boats" [that is, narrow boats, see p.234], large numbers of which were moored off the different wharfs abutting on the canal, and cautioned them to be on the alert for their own security. .... a few minutes before 4 o'clock a loud noise was heard to the north of the town which momentarily approached nearer and nearer, and it was soon ascertained that the narrow stream of the Brent had swelled into a mighty river, and overflowing its banks, was pouring itself into the already increased waters of the canal. Numbers of boats, barges and lighters were instantly

torn from their moorings, and driven with great force through the bridge towards the Thames. At the same instant, also, the accumulated waters having overflowed all the premises north of the high-road burst with frightful force through two avenues... near the bridge....'

In fact it seems that the sudden rush of water resulted from the fracture of one of the dams on the Brent (Welsh Harp) Reservoir. Four persons died in the flood, and an enormous amount of damage was done both to watercraft and to houses close to the canal bank. Many were rendered homeless, and many of these slept on straw in the Infants School in the Butts until their dwellings could be dried out. The waterway along here was filled with wrecked and sunken barges and other craft.

Keep walking down the ramp and onto the road. Where you go under a narrow road bridge (in fact, an 1876 railway bridge, now adapted for road traffic) **turn sharp left, back to the riverbank.**

A variety of craft are moored along this stretch.

Persevere along the path, but after passing a large timber yard shed followed by housing with a communal lawn, <u>watch out to take metal steps</u> down onto the lower terrace where the houseboats are moored. Otherwise you will not reach the steps back up to the High Street.

This part of Brentford was once known as the Ham – a 'hamm' in Anglo-Saxon denoted a piece of land enclosed by a winding river – in this case, by the Brent. For about a century, from 1750, most of the land here was a nursery run by the Ronalds family. By 1830 Hugh Ronalds, the younger, was growing over 300 varieties of apple here and in 1831 published his treatise, *Pyrus Malus Brentfordiensis*.

On reaching the High Street.

On this part of the High Street a Civil War battle was fought. The Parliamentarians believed they had a truce and were negotiating with King Charles at Colnbrook on 11 November 1642. However, the following day Royalists advanced from Hounslow Heath and attacked the small force holding the bridge at Brentford in order to advance on London. A Royalist wrote as follows:

> 'unexpectedly we were encountered by two or three regiments of theirs, who had made some small barricades at the end of the first town called New-Braineford [roughly where Syon's Lion Gate now stands]. The van of our army being about 1000 musketeers, answered their shot so bitterly, that within an hour or less they forsook their work in that place, and fled up to another which they had raised betwixt the two towns....[here at the bridge] My Colonel's regiment was the sixth that was brought to assault, after 5 others had all discharged, whose happy honour it was (assisted by God, and a new piece of canon newly come up) to drive them from that work too, where it was an heart-breaking object to hear and see the most miserable deaths of many goodly men.... And [we] took 400 prisoners. But what was most pitiful was, to see how many poor men ended and lost their lives, striving to save them; for they run into the Thames, and about 200 of them, as we might judge, were there drowned by themselves, and so were guilty of their own deaths; for had they stayed, and yielded up themselves, the king's mercy is so gracious, that he had spared them all.'

One may be justifiably sceptical regarding the last remark. Captured soldiers were threatened with branding if they did not change sides. Meanwhile Prince Rupert ordered Brentford to be sacked 'as a punishment for having attached itself to the side of the rebels'. So, in time-dishonoured fashion, the Royalists first got their hands on the liquor and then stole everything they could, destroying all the fishermen's boats and nets and thus their livelihood. Such was the hardship caused that Brentford was still in receipt of relief a decade later. As for the Royalists, they were repulsed by an estimated 24,000 men at Turnham Green the following day. It could hardly have helped their chances that they were still badly hung-over. They never again got so close to London.

Turn left, across the bridge.

A bridge has been here for about 800 years. In about 1280 Edward I applied a toll on this bridge on all cattle, merchandise and also on all Jews: those on horseback one penny (£1.70 in today's money), those on foot a halfpenny.

Follow the main road for 300 metres and turn left for the pedestrian entrance into Syon Park.

It will come as no surprise that this is an old track into Syon which, like the road through Brentford itself, many people have tramped along over the centuries. Look out on your left for glimpses of the great Conservatory, designed by Charles Fowler for the 3rd, swimming, Duke in 1827. You may already be familiar with Fowler's work. He designed the covered market for Covent Garden. The central palm house of the conservatory has a steep curvilinear dome, designed to maximise the direct transmission of the sun's rays, following the theory of the great nineteenth century horti-culturalist, John Loudon. The ribs of the dome are made of the alloy gunmetal (copper and zinc).

Follow the carriageway through Syon Park.

On your right, dead ground in the arcadian fields hides the serpentine lake, which follows the rough path of the old river channel that once, 500 years ago or more, rendered most of Syon Park an ait. The lake was dug by Capability Brown as part of his new landscape, but you will spot a small arched footbridge. It is in the spirit of Brown that cattle still peacefully graze.

Turn left at the far end of the Park. Follow the road, Church Street, past the church.

Note the gothicised Butterfield House, the recent (1971) and highly successful fraud you viewed from the Surrey bank (p.51). One can only admire its cheek. Next door stands No. 61, early nineteenth century with its delightful balcony and upper pilasters inspired by Soane's work. Richard Reynolds House is Georgian.

Just after the traffic constraint but before the bridge, turn left at the tastefully engraved 'Riverside Walk' plaque.

You will find yourself crossing the Duke of Northumberland's river, first cut in the mid-sixteenth century to improve the water power for the mills sited in the village. Modern apartment buildings have replaced the old mills and wharves of this once busy river port. In half a century Isleworth has moved from working port to commuter neighbourhood.

Admire the workshops on the muddy foreshore of Isleworth Ait. Such workshops, like those on Lot's Ait, Brentford, may be at risk from newly arrived residents of this historically industrial part of the Thames who object to the hammering necessary in a boatyard. How do we want our Thames? Silent or working? The ait is also home to 57 varieties of bird life and the double-lipped door snail, which is virtually unique to this stretch of the Thames. The osier beds are still harvested (see p.223).

Continue past the *Town Wharf* pub until Thames Path signs compel you to turn right, inland. Turn left at the mini roundabout and follow the main Richmond Road.

Nazareth House was built in 1832 for George III's chaplain. Then it became a convent. Now shut up, it is hardly prepossessing but the high wall and 1893 chapel built for the convent give it an air of secrecy.

Endure the traffic for about 300 metres, and having crossed the unassuming bridge over the river Crane, turn left along the quiet cul-de-sac, Railshead Road, back to the river footpath past the front of Gordon House.

The rest of this walk back to Richmond may retrace the route back into Richmond (reverse the instructions from p.26 or cross the Richmond lock, p.29).

➡ Kew Green. Pause, as you emerge onto Kew Green at the corner of Bush Road.

Kew Green is the relic of part of the medieval manorial waste. So close to the river it was probably largely water meadow, devoted principally to the pasturing of livestock, the gleaning of firewood and perhaps the removal of turf for roofing peasant hovels. From the sixteenth century, however, an increasing number of grants were made of small parcels of land around the edge of this common waste, many to courtiers, since it was conveniently close to the palace in Richmond. Initially these land grants were at the west end, which had once stretched all the way to the Brentford Ferry (roughly by the car park upstream). By the late eighteenth century the Green was largely as we see it today. Some rebuilding has taken place but the principal shape was already established, and many of the early eighteenth century houses still survive. During the late nineteenth century, with the huge popularity of Kew Gardens as a day resort, the houses along the north side, with their gardens running down to the Thames, were almost all devoted to providing refreshments and food for visitors.

Turn right. You may care to note various houses listed below as you promenade around the edge of the Green but do not let all these details spoil your enjoyment of the Green.

No. 83, Capel House on the corner of Bush Road, and No. 77 are both c. 1720.

The central part of the **Herbarium** is Robert Hunter's old house, before it passed into royal hands.

The **main gates to Kew Gardens** were designed by Decimus Burton in 1846, superceding four successive gates from Kew Green.

Nos. 53-55 are early Georgian, No. 55 may even date back to the 1690s.

No. 51 was created out of two Georgian dwellings, in one of which lived Charlotte Papendiek, 'reader' to George III's consort, Queen Charlotte. Her journal was published a century later, in 1887.

No 49 has been the Gardens' director's official residence since 1851.

Nos. 45-39 the Gables, was built for the Gardens' staff in 1908. The ornamental gables were copied from the stables previously standing here.

No. 33 was once Lord Bute's family residence, but in the nineteenth century became the home of the Duke of Cambridge and acquired the name of Cambridge Cottage.

No. 35 (or 37?) was once 'Lord Bute's study'. This was the subject of scurrilous comment, for it was widely believed that he was having an affair with the widowed Princess Augusta (on Bute and Augusta, see p. 85). A drawing published in the *Political Register* in 1767 showed this house, captioned 'where none of his family resides', distinctly apart from No 33, his family's residence. A path was shown to run from the back of Lord Bute's study into the royal gardens and thus to Princess Augusta. The whole drawing was saucily entitled 'A View of Lord Bute's Erections at Kew'. George III, Augusta's son, had the house off him five years later, in 1772.

On your left

St Anne's Church on the Green is a charming architectural mess. Built originally as a chapel to serve the hamlet during Queen Anne's reign (and tactfully dedicated to St Anne), it had 24 pews, sufficient to accommodate 90 souls. Completed in 1714, it was lengthened in 1770 and a north aisle added. In 1805 a new west front including the portico and a south aisle were built. In 1851 the apse-like mausoleum, for the Duke of Cambridge after he had fulfilled his allotted days, was plonked on the east end but in 1884 it was moved further east to accommodate a new chancel.

On your right

No. 29 was built c. 1726.

No. 25 was owned by one of the Hilliers, the family of watermen, who leased it to Thomas Gainsborough, duly buried in St Anne's churchyard.

Nos 19-17, Gumley Cottage dates back to 1717.

Kew Gardens in the Eighteenth Century

Distance 3.5 km: 2 hours

This walk covers the historical landscape of the Gardens, after which the rest awaits your own investigations. There are plenty of refreshment places to take breaks. You will get all and more than your money's worth by exploring the historical landscape and then visiting the museum and glasshouses, but come early on a fine day.

NOTE: If you wish to see the interior of Queen Charlotte's cottage, it is open annually every May Day bank holiday.

BEFORE YOU WALK

Originally, what we now know as Kew Gardens was two separate strips of land either side of Love Lane (see sketch map, p.86). The older one, Richmond Gardens, ran along the riverbank from the present Old Deer Park in Richmond to Kew. Its nucleus was James I's hunting park, elongated towards Kew as further plots were incorporated during the first half of the eighteenth century. James I's old hunting lodge had been converted into a small palace by William III. Following his death in 1702, a lease was taken by the Duke of Ormonde, a dashing and popular general. Ormonde made major improvements but destroyed the chance to enjoy his handiwork. He did not approve of the Hanoverian succession and in June 1715 he was impeached. He fled to France and following the collapse of the Old Pretender's rebellion, thought it wise to stay away from Britain for a very long time. (He made a highly successful return as a corpse, to be buried in Westminster Abbey in the year of the Young Pretender's rebellion, 30 years later.) In the meantime his estate was forfeit and George, to become II but still Prince, and Caroline, his consort, moved into Ormonde Lodge in 1718, renaming it Richmond Lodge. They had badly needed to get away from Westminster, since the prince was on such bad terms with his father, George I, a tradition faithfully continued throughout the Hanoverian dynasty. Caroline acquired and developed extra plots of land at the northern end of the estate, so that by her death in 1737 she had occupancy of almost everything between Love Lane and the river. At the far northern end, and on the far side of Love Lane, Caroline also acquired the Dutch House, now known as Kew Palace, with which this walk commences.

The other estate, Kew Gardens, was started in the 1730s. It contained the original botanical garden. It, too, was increased piecemeal. It ran parallel to Richmond Gardens on its inland side but was separated from it by Love Lane, a public footpath to Richmond (finally closed in 1785 and eradicated in 1802). On its east side it was bordered by the present main road from Kew to Richmond. It was the home of George and Caroline's son, Frederick and his consort Augusta, who lived in the White House, at the north end of the garden. It is these two gardens which this walk is intended to re-create in the mind's eye.

By the second half of the eighteenth century the two gardens had features in common, principally the idea of setting follies in among the foliage to create a whimsical landscape. Kew Gardens, however, was very much the more interesting, for it was here that the botanical garden was first created in the 1750s. Although this walk is intended to remain firmly focussed on the eighteenth century, I must confess to a number of deviations *en route*, which I am not sufficiently strong-minded to ignore.

A VERY BRIEF NOTE ON HOW KEW BECAME SERIOUSLY BOTANICAL

Until the end of the eighteenth century the botanical part of the gardens remained very small. The much more extensive pleasure grounds were intended to be both entertaining and productive. They afforded grazing for sheep and cattle. Pheasants were reared. Down near the Pagoda cereal crops grew. One head gardener, William Aiton, was expected to produce substantial fruits from his trees. Indeed, he did just that. In 1810 he produced no fewer than 200 baskets of figs for the royal table. This, one must remember, was the productive estate of George III, 'Farmer' George, a man at his happiest when breeding sheep. Botany was still a sideline.

Nevertheless, in the last 30 years of the eighteenth century the gardens rapidly began to acquire a reputation for their botanical collection. The driving force behind this process was Joseph Banks, a wealthy young man from Lincolnshire who had paid for eight others and himself to join Captain Cooke's HMS *Endeavour* in 1768 on its secret voyage to Australia and the Pacific. The ostensible purpose of the voyage was to track the transit of Venus from the Pacific in the following year, which keenly interested George III (see p.46). Banks returned in 1771, a famous man for his collection of botanical and zoological specimens. Enjoying the royal esteem, he quietly assumed a directing position at Kew Gardens. Until his death in 1820, Banks managed to cajole a large number of travellers to bring back specimens from exotic places for Kew. Indeed he importuned generals, admirals, merchants, missionaries and anyone else he could lay hands on, people who had never before looked a leaf in the eye, so to speak, to assist Kew in the collection of specimens. The East India Company went out of its way to help, simply on the basis of his intercessions. He also commissioned collectors, like Archibald Menzies (who features below), who brought back monkey-puzzle seedlings. It is a tribute to Banks' own charm and the friendship and the esteem in which he was held, that his efforts made Kew the world's leading botanical garden. Without Banks, Kew might easily have become like Kensington Gardens or Hyde Park, pleasurable but without the least influence on botany or ecology.

Wherever you enter Kew Gardens, ensure you receive a free modern map of the gardens at the ticket office. Once it is open to the public, you should consider purchasing a ticket to cover entry to Kew Palace (the Dutch House) also.

Enter the Gardens by either

(a) **Brentford Gate (car park). Follow signs to the White Peaks café, noting a few of the manifold varieties of eucalyptus as you pass. Walk around the front of the café and make for the sundial on the greensward and then for Kew Palace, the red brick building behind it;**

(b) **The main gate (closest to Kew Bridge Station). Keep straight, passing the floral 'roundabout' and following the tarmac path that leads to Kew Palace; or**

(c) **Victoria Gate (Kew Gardens Station). The worst option, since you must map-read yourself to Kew Palace.**

Kew Palace, better described as the Dutch House, was built by a London merchant of Flemish origin in 1631 (the initials S&C F over the doorway standing for Samuel and Catherine Fortrey, who built it). It stood on the lane to Brentford ferry, still visible crossing the approach to the house as the tarmac carriageway running through wrought iron gates next to the old stable building (on the left as you face the Dutch House). Caroline, consort of George II, rented the house in 1728 as a residence for her daughters until they married. Much later, in 1753, George II installed his grandson, George, Prince of Wales. Once king, George III and his consort Charlotte initiated the royal habit of living two lives, the one of public appearances and the other – the one they much preferred – of private domesticity. They lived at the White House (see below) till 1802, and then moved to the Dutch House as a *pied à terre* while the new palace on the riverbank (see p.58) was being built.

Its principal outward claim on your interest, however, is that this 'Netherlands style' town house became popular among the wealthier classes of London in the 1630s. City craftsmen, notably bricklayers, drew their inspiration from Netherlands pattern books with a distinctly Dutch version of classicism. This combined the Jacobean tradition of gables and mullioned windows with carved brick and the celebration of the classical orders. The style is now rare, with only a handful of surviving examples. The brickwork is Flemish bond (see p.246), very much an innovation in England at the time. (Your chance to admire English bond will come at the Ice House.) One can see that the bricklayers who built this house had done their homework: rustication around the windows, refined pilasters on the central bay. They also tried to enhance the appearance of the brickwork, by running the edge of a penny through the wet mortar ('penny-struck') to create the illusion of thin mortar as on the finest brickwork of the day. Sash windows replaced the original brick mullions early on. (Destroying original windows has been a ghastly habit ever since.) The double curved 'Dutch' gables and pediments and the classical pilasters of the central bay demonstrate an awareness of the Renaissance that at this juncture one would have had great difficulty finding in the provinces, where Tudor styles still prevailed. Sadly the ground floor entrance pilasters, with Doric capitals, were removed in the early nineteenth century. Above, however, the Ionic and Corinthian capitals testify to the newly acquired grammar of classicism.

Most of the interior of the house, as restored, belongs to the time of George III and, when it is open to the public, merits a close look either now or after this walk.

Go around the left side to the rear of the house.

The garden, laid out between 1969 and 1975, is a pastiche of a Stuart garden, far too crowded for so confined a space. But it merits more than a glance, since its features are copied or adopted from contemporary gardens. Here are essential features of a Stuart garden. Straight ahead lies a sunken garden planted with sweet smelling and medicinal plants. It is surrounded by alleys of pleached laburnum, a tree introduced to Britain from southern Europe in c.1560. To your right lies the central garden with a small pool, a parterre of beds of lavender, rosemary and santolina bordered with box hedges. It is directly comparable with the Cherry Garden at Ham House. The north end is enclosed by the curved hedge, lined with five surviving 'terms' or busts, originally commissioned in about 1734 by Frederick, Prince of Wales for his own garden a couple of hundred metres away, at the White House (see below). This enclosed end testifies to the standard absence of vista from the house. It was only in the middle of the century that the idea of a view from the house through the garden to countryside beyond started to catch on, as Francis Bacon's essay on gardens, dated 1597 (see p.247), became better known. At the rear of the house, the arcade *loggia* is not original but it is accurately reinstated. Cross the central garden and inspect the 'mount' beyond, a popular feature in both Tudor and Stuart times from which to view surrounding gardens. At its foot runs a short walk of hornbeam, elegantly clipped according to the then current style.

The White House.

Follow the hornbeam walk out and make for the sundial on the greensward.

This is where the White House once stood, perhaps the most important dwelling ever in the gardens, or to be more exact 'Kew Gardens' as opposed to Queen Caroline's 'Richmond Gardens', along the river front. The White House was remodelled after its acquisition by Caroline's son, Frederick, Prince of Wales in 1731.

The house already had a horticultural pedigree, for it had been inhabited by Sir Henry Capel. The diarist John Evelyn, who shared this passion, had gone there in 1678 and described it:

> 'it is an old timber house; but his garden has the choicest fruit of any plantation in England, as he is most industrious and understanding in it.'

On another visit a decade later he noted:

> 'From thence [William Temple's house, not far from the

present Kew Observatory in West Sheen] to Kew, to visit
Sir Henry Capell's, whose orangery and myrtetum [myrtle
house] are most beautiful and perfectly well kept. He was
contriving very high pallisades of reeds to shade his oranges
during the summer, and painting those reeds in oil.'

It was probably the first orangery in England. The house passed
to Sir Henry's grandniece, Elizabeth Capel, wife of Samuel
Molyneux, of whom more below.

Back to poor Prince Frederick. It seems almost unbelievable, but
his own mother loathed him. Queen Caroline had told a friend that
Frederick was:

'the greatest ass, and the greatest liar, and the greatest
canaille [scoundrel], and the greatest beast in the whole
world, and... I most heartily wished he were out of it.'

It is questionable whether any of this was true to his real
character and the last phrase could only mean she wished her son
dead. Indeed, so much did she hate him that even on her deathbed
she refused to see him. So the great mystery is why on earth
Frederick, who could have been under no illusions about his loveless
upbringing, chose to obtain a house barely 100 metres in front of the
'Red [Dutch] House' that his mother had acquired only three years
earlier. Was it a desperate attempt to gain her affection? Or, more
probably, a defiant poke in the eye, since the White House marred
the view from the Dutch House?

Frederick wasted no time making the place his own. In 1729 he
gave William Kent (see p.251) his very first building commission,
to enlarge the house and reface both the north and south fronts as a
Palladian mansion. Frederick died suddenly in his early 50s in
March 1751, probably from an internal abscess, which possibly
resulted from a sporting injury. He left a widow, Princess Augusta
of Saxe-Gotha, not known for her cleverness. Yet she was shrewd
enough to ensure she never posed any threat to her parents-in-law

and that the odium endured by her husband never fell upon her. After her own death in 1772, her son George III and his consort Charlotte moved into the White House but demolished it in 1802 while George was gripped by his projected castellated folly on the riverbank.

You will be wondering about the sundial. It marks important astronomical discoveries (if you do not wish to know more, skip to the next paragraph). In the 1720s the (later White) house had been occupied by George [II] Prince of Wales' secretary, Samuel Molyneux, a dedicated astronomer, married to Elizabeth Capel. With his friend, an Anglican clergyman, James Bradley, he set up a telescope in the house. Molyneux died in 1728, but that year Bradley announced his discovery of the aberration of starlight. From his observations of the annual changes in stellar position since 1725, he concluded that the apparent stellar shift was attributable to an aberration of light, the result of the finite speed of light and the forward motion of the Earth in its orbit. There was more to come. He also realised that this hypothesis failed to explain a shift in some of the fixed stars. He concluded that this was caused by the annual 'nutation' or very slight uneven nodding motion of the Earth's axis, a result of the changing gravitational pull of the Moon. Because it took 18.6 years for the Moon to complete its precessional (like the wobble of a spinning top) orbit around the Earth, Bradley patiently monitored the complete orbit before announcing his discovery in 1748. Say what you will about the eighteenth century Church of England, it gave space for its clerics to study the natural world.

Perhaps you set out on this walk with the sole purpose of being told which is the largest tree at Kew. In which case you need go no further. It is the bulky and handsome chestnut leafed oak, 50 metres ahead and slightly left of you. It has the largest mass of all the trees at Kew. This one, from the Caucasus, arrived in 1846, the very first of its kind to come to Britain. It has probably still not quite reached its fullest extent. A little to its left is an Oriental Plane, a species

The Lake, with its Swan Boat, made for George Prince of Wales' 17th birthday in 1755. The White House is in the distance and, on the left, the Temple of Arethusa before it was moved to its present location. It is a royal theme park that makes Disneyworld seem passé.

introduced to Britain in the mid-sixteenth century. You will already be wondering why the ground below these trees appears bare. In fact almost all the older trees at Kew are surrounded by a mulch to encourage the growth of mycorrhizal fungi, the underground network of fungal filaments (see p.258). It has recently been found that mycorrhizal fungi and tree roots enjoy an important symbiotic relationship, but we are still on the nursery slopes of understanding the complexities of ecosystems.

Before moving on: In front of the White House an enormous lake was dug, leaving a large island, in the early 1750s. It stretched easily as far as the present Palm House. It is from here that one may imagine the promenade, in fact a serious walk, taken by Princess Augusta's guests to the far end of the garden and back.

Turn left and walk along the front of the Orangery.

Princess Augusta commissioned William Chambers to build the Orangery in 1757. He applied a special stucco which he promised would endure. And so it has. In the two pediments of the façade a large monogram 'A' ensures no one forgets who built it. Over the central door is her married escutcheon, bearing witness to an astonishing armorial appetite that lays claim to Great Britain, Ireland, France and a clutch of Germanic states. By 1769 the Orangery was 'filled completely, chiefly with oranges which bear extremely well and large.' But the praise was perhaps too fulsome. The roof rendered the building too dark for its purpose. It is much more successful as a teahouse.

Frederick and Augusta were serious about botany, and it is to them and yet more to their hyper-enthusiastic friend, James Stuart, Earl of Bute, that Kew owes its botanical origins. Bute had already started a collection of exotic plants on his island in the Firth of Clyde. Frederick shared his interest, but it was Augusta who really started collecting in earnest in 1759. Unlike her mother-in-law, Caroline, whose garden was devoted to vistas and architectural surprises, Augusta had a dedicated botanical garden, close to the house. Three of the earliest plants still survive.

Continue along the tarmac path beyond the Orangery.

On your right you will pass a young monkey-puzzle tree. Monkey-puzzles are native to Chile and Argentina. Discovered by a Spaniard in 1780, five seedlings were brought back to Britain in 1795, at least one of which came to Kew where it eventually died in 1892. It had been reared against the odds by Archibald Menzies, surgeon and naturalist aboard HMS *Discovery*. Menzies first had to acquire a seed of the tree. He was dining with the Spanish governor of Chile, who had refused him permission to explore the land, when he noticed the seeds in his dessert. Was this a test or a tease? Did the

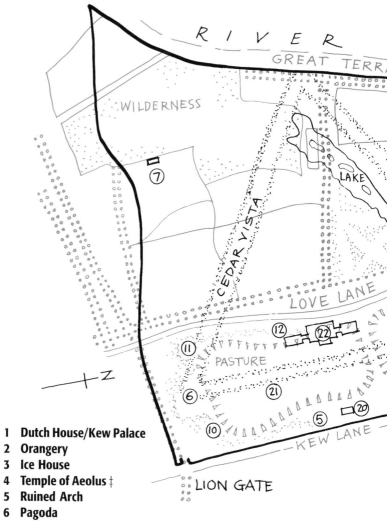

1 **Dutch House/Kew Palace**
2 **Orangery**
3 **Ice House**
4 **Temple of Aeolus** ‡
5 **Ruined Arch**
6 **Pagoda**
7 **Queen Charlotte's Cottage**
8 Temple of Bellona *
9 Lake †
10 Alhambra †
11 Mosque †
12 Gothic Cathedral †

13 Temple of Arethusa *
14 White House †
15 Temple of the Sun †
16 Princess Augusta's Physic or
   Exotic Garden †

KEW GARDENS 21st Century

RICHMOND GARDENS AND KEW GARDENS 18th Century

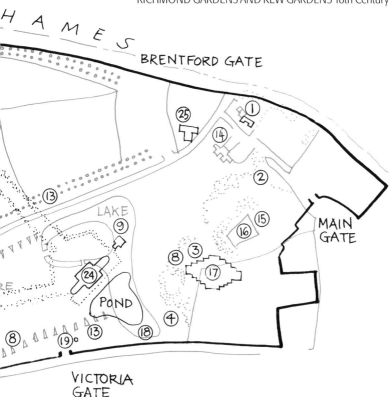

17	**Princess of Wales Conservatory**	24	**Palm House**
18	**Plants and People Exhibition**	25	**White Peaks**
19	**Campanile**		
20	**Marianne North Gallery**		
21	**Pavilion Restaurant**		
22	**Temperate House**		
23	**King William's Temple**		

governor expect Menzies to exclaim, "Aha! *Auracaria araucana!*" as he gazed into his dessert? Whether Menzies risked a dangerous breach of etiquette by pocketing them at the dinner table or whether he dutifully swallowed them whole only to retrieve them later, he acquired his seeds. His next, and arguably greater, peril was the animosity of the ship's captain, George Vancouver, who disliked having plants aboard his ship. Vancouver ran the ultimate tight ship. When Menzies complained of the loss of some of his plants in their frames on the quarterdeck as a consequence of his assistant being assigned to nautical duties, Vancouver placed him under arrest. The germination and survival of five monkey-puzzle seedlings is therefore something of a miracle.

At the next tarmac crossing turn right.

Set back from the path a few paces off on your right is a large tree, the locust tree or *Robinia pseudoacacia*, bound together at the base by an iron band. It is on its last legs. It was planted by Princess Augusta in 1759 and is thus the oldest survivor of her collection. The robinia or false acacia was introduced to England from the New World in the 1630s and is now a common sight in suburban gardens. There was a craze for the robinia in the early nineteenth century thanks to William Cobbett's vigorous promotion of the wood's resistance to decay, following his visit to America in 1818:

> 'The durability of this wood is such, that no man in America will pretend to say that he ever saw a bit of it in a decayed state.'

He sold it as better than oak for ships and houses, indeed that it was a wonder tree. The tree was already known in Britain as 'robinia' but Cobbett promoted it using the American name of 'locust tree'. Almost no one knew that the two trees were one and the same, and Cobbett chose not to disabuse them. As the credulous sought to invest, Cobbett bought up more than a million robinia saplings from nurserymen across Britain and sold them at a substantial profit. The tree proved insufficiently straight to be of any use for ships or houses but by then Cobbett had made a tidy profit.

A few paces on your left once stood Chamber's Corinthian Temple of the Sun, the first of a series of kiosks demonstrating mastery of the classical orders. Built in 1761, it imitated the Temple of Venus at Baalbek in the Lebanon. Much of it was made of plaster, not strong enough to stand up to the cedar of Lebanon which spectacularly fell on it in 1916, a minor demon-  stration of that lovely country's tragic gift for self-destruction. If you wish to see an almost exact contemporary copy of the Baalbek temple, visit the Temple of Apollo at Stourhead, Wilts. Both, like many of their contemporaries, were inspired by the illustrations of the Huguenot Jean Marot (father of Daniel, see vol I. p. 92), who had visited and drawn the temples at Baalbek a century earlier.

A few paces on, on your right: you will find another important part of Augusta's botanical collection, the Maidenhead or *Gingko Biloba* tree. This particular tree is probably the first ever to come to Britain and was first planted by Archibald 3rd Duke of Argyll in his *arboretum* at Whitton. When he died in 1761, it was acquired for Kew probably by Bute, Argyll's nephew. The *Gingko* is remarkable because it is an 'early primitive' tree, in existence at the time of dinosaurs, 180-200 million years ago.

A couple more paces, on your right: the wisteria first came to Britain in 1816. All the original introductions were cuttings from one plant growing in the garden of a Chinese merchant in Canton. This wisteria is about 150 years old.

About 100 metres on, on your left: this ancient pagoda tree, *sophora japonica*, was one of the first five brought to England from China in 1753. It probably came to Kew via Argyll's *arboretum* at Whitton in about 1763. Despite its strong purgative properties, the Chinese were not shy of adulterating opium with the ground wood of this tree.

Veer left and turn to the left to see the Ice House.

The icehouse probably dates from the digging of the lake, which presumably provided the ice. It has been filled in, and must have been about four metres deep. (On icehouses, see vol. 1, p.83) The brick is laid in English bond, by the 1750s a disappearing style of bricklaying (see p.246).

Turn left on leaving the icehouse.

On your right you pass an enormous weeping beech.

Pass across the front of the Princess of Wales' Conservatory. Veer to the right to pass around the left side of the Mound.

Along the foot of this knoll in spring there is a riot of blue shades: chionadoxas and scillas and their hybrids. At the top of the mound you will see the Temple of Aeolus. It was designed by William Chambers and rebuilt, mercifully in stone, by Decimus Burton. As for Aeolus, he was Zeus' guardian of the winds. He lived on an island paradise north of Sicily. To this island came Odysseus and his men on their long way back to Ithaca from Troy. Aeolus helped

Odysseus by giving him all the boisterous winds sewn up in a leather bag and leaving outside the gentle west wind to waft Odysseus back to Ithaca. But while he slept his crew, thinking the bag contained treasure, opened it. As Homer recounts, this was definitely a bad idea.

Continue around the Mound and turn left to pass the front of the *Plants and People Exhibition* (which is wonderful). Resist it if you can, until the end of the walk.

On your right, the pond is the last vestige of the great lake created by Frederick and Augusta. The two tall swamp cypresses (coyly hiding their root 'knees' under ground ivy) do not date back to the original garden (they were planted in 1846). It is very likely that they had predecessors in Kew Gardens, since the swamp cypress had been introduced to England in the mid seventeenth century.

As the path bears around to the left, look out for the modest Ionic Temple of Arethusa (1758) by William Chambers on your left, moved from its original location on the far side of the then much larger lake. It is still appropriately sited by the water. Arethusa was a wood nymph who bathed in the river Alpheus. The god of the river greatly fancied her but Artemis (Diana) intervened to protect her from his saucy advances by turning her into a spring.

This so far has been roughly the route of Princess Augusta's garden tour for her guests, but no longer. Straight ahead stands an obstacle and a distraction from the eighteenth century landscape: Decimus Burton's Romanesque campanile, built in the 1840s. It is really a chimney, built to serve the 12 boilers underneath the Palm House. It also housed a water tank near its top, filled by a steam-driven pump, thus providing pressured water to spray even the tallest trees in the Palm House. Burton was also primarily responsible for the great Palm House. The end of this walk brings you back to the Palm House. It is a great triumph of the Victorian era, the equivalent to a gothic cathedral and posing similar engineering problems. As with a great cathedral, one feels privileged to enter it.

Turn right.

You may note a couple of small manhole covers in the lawn to your right. They mark the subterranean tunnel whereby coke was wheeled from the campanile to the boilers under the Palm House. The light seeping through these covers is the only form of lighting in the tunnel. In winter this tunnel often flooded, to the extreme distress of those moving the coke. Exposing the public to the unsightly reality of coke, however, was not an option in those prim times. For Kew's students a walk through the tunnel remains an initiation rite. The Palm House itself was periodically fumigated in the nineteenth century by burning off piles of contraband tobacco impounded by HM Customs and Excise.

Turn left along the main avenue, past the Victoria Gate.

On your right, facing onto the greensward stands Chambers' Temple of Bellona (1760). Chambers, or his patron, was anxious to demonstrate his mastery of the classical orders. This temple is of the Doric order. Bellona, as her name implies, was the Roman personification of bloody warfare. The inside walls bear plaques to the various British and Hanoverian regiments which had distinguished themselves in the bloodletting of the Seven Years War. (If you later chance on King William's Temple, it too was built to commemorate the victories between 1759 and 1837.)

Cleave to the path – yes, Princess Augusta's – parallel and close to Kew Road to arrive at the Flagpole.

The plaque on the path tells one everything one needs to know about the flagpole.

Continue walking along the path.

On your left you will pass another nineteenth century deviation: the Marianne North Gallery, devoted entirely to the paintings of Miss North. She only began her travels in 1871 at the age of 40, but visited Latin America, the Caribbean, south east Asia, the Far East and finally Africa. She offered Kew Gardens not only her substantial collection of paintings but also a suitable gallery to house them, designed by her friend James Fergusson, who had lived and worked in India. The gallery is suitably suggestive of India with its verandah. Enter it to have your mind boggled more by Miss North's assiduity than by her art. There is something very Victorian in her thoroughness. Some plants she painted are now extinct.

Continue walking to the Ruined Arch.

Follies, or noble ruins, appealed to the English gentry of the eighteenth century, a reminder that *sic transit gloria mundi*. Chambers built this one in 1760, as he put it, 'a Roman antiquity built of brick with incrustation of stone.' This, however, was a folly with a practical purpose: a bridge across the path, as an access route from Kew lane (now Road) for the livestock that were grazed in the central pasture to render it truly Arcadian. One might want to gaze upon the creatures of Arcadia, but one certainly did not wish to tangle with them or, indeed, with their droppings. This pasture and another, abutting the lake, were enclosed with a ha-ha to convey the impression of an uninterrupted landscape.

It must have been somewhere around here that Fanny Burney had her surprising and somewhat discomfiting encounter with the demented King George III one February morning in 1789.

Either find a seat to read it now or save till later her record of what took place:

'This morning, when I received my intelligence of the King, from Dr John Willis, I begged to know where I might walk in safety? In Kew Gardens, he said, as the King would be in Richmond [Gardens]… Everybody, indeed is ordered to keep out of sight [of the King]….

I had proceeded, in my quick way, nearly half the round, when I suddenly perceived, through some Trees, two or three figures…. I concluded them to be workmen, and Gardeners; – yet tried to look sharp, – and in so doing, as they were less shaded, I thought I saw the person of his Majesty!

Alarmed past all possible expression, I waited not to know more, but turning back, ran off with all my might – But what was my terror to hear myself pursued! – to hear the voice of the King himself, loudly and hoarsely calling after me "Miss Burney! Miss Burney! –"

I protest I was ready to die;… I knew not what state he might be in at the time;… Nevertheless, on I ran, - too terrified to stop …..

Heavens how I ran! I do not think I should have felt the hot Lava from Vesuvius, – at least not the hot Cinders, had I so ran during its Eruption. My feet were not sensible that they even touched the Ground.

Soon after, I heard other voices, shriller though less nervous, call out "Stop! Stop! – Stop! –"

I could by no means consent, – I knew not what was purposed…. Still, therefore, on I flew – and such was my speed, so almost incredible to relate, or recollect, that I fairly believe no one of the whole party could have overtaken me, if these words, from one of the Attendants had not reached me "Dr Willis begs you to stop! –"

"I cannot! — I cannot!—" I answered, still flying on, — when he called out "You *must*, ma'am, it hurts the King to run. —" Then indeed I stopt!….

When they were within a few yards of me, the King called out "Why did you run away? —" …. I looked up and met all his wonted benignity of Countenance, though something still of wildness in his Eyes. Think, however, of my surprise, to feel him put both his Hands round my two shoulders and then kiss my Cheek! — I wonder I did not really sink, so exquisite was my affright when I saw him spread out his arms.

Involuntarily, I concluded he meant to crush me…. I have reason, however, to believe it was but joy of a Heart unbridled, now, by the forms and proprieties of established custom, and sober Reason. He looked almost in *rapture* at the meeting, from the moment I advanced…He now spoke in such terms of his pleasure in seeing me, that I soon lost the whole of my terror…… What a scene! How variously was I affected by it! — but, upon the whole, how inexpressibly thankful to see him so nearly himself!'

Continue walking, but veer right and make for the Pagoda.

It was here at the farthest extremity from the White House that Princess Augusta's guests came upon one oriental fantasy after another. Only the Pagoda remains. Originally however, there was an Alhambra, an imagined Moorish pavilion, bearing only a faint resemblance to the real thing. It was too flimsy to last and was demolished in 1820.

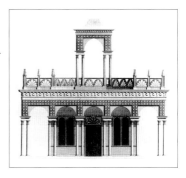

Then came the Pagoda, the sole survivor, built in 1761. It was not the first 'pagoda' in England but it rapidly became the most famous. It took only a few months to run up. Gilded dragons stood poised on the extremities of roofs, ready for takeoff, and the balconies were painted red and blue. But for all its chinoiserie, it remains stolidly British, with its ponderous tower and Georgian windows complete with fanlights, all completely unrecognisable to anyone from China. The brickwork was necessary to achieve the height. Remarkably, the brickwork has endured unblemished, a tribute to the solid foundation and fine bricklaying.

Turn hard right at the Pagoda, to walk down the so-called 'Cedar Vista', marked on the Gardens map.

The Cedar Vista is a Victorian imposition on the previous landscape. A brief word on pines and cedars, since you will pass both. There are at least 80 varieties of pine. If you are interested in the rural landscape (but it won't help at all in Kew) Scots pines disappeared from all Britain except Scotland 5,000 years ago. But since the eighteenth century and possibly earlier, they were deliberately planted in many parts of Britain.

Now for cedars. There are only four varieties, of which the cedar of Lebanon is the most famous and earliest arrival in Britain (1638). Two other varieties are also Mediterranean: the Atlas, Atlantic or Algerian cedar (1841) and the rare Cyprus cedar (1879). The Deodar came from the Himalayas in 1831. If you wish to identify them there is a simple rule: look carefully at the *young tips* of branches and follow the alliterative rubric: Atlas *ascend*, Lebanon are *level*, and Deodar *descend*. Look at anything but the youngest tips, however, and one comes badly unstuck. So it is much safer to read the labels.

On your left. Look out for the Japanese landscape garden with its dwarf Gateway of the Imperial Messenger, a relic of the Japan-Britain Exhibition of 1910. Given all the other inanimate exotics created at Kew, it has definitely come to the right place. Moreover, it stands on the knoll where once Chambers' cod-Ottoman mosque stood. Like the Alhambra, the 'mosque' was far too flimsy to last more than two or three decades. Its interior had nothing to do with

Islam but consisted of a bright yellow rococo chamber, the dome supported on eight green stucco palm trees, a kind of lath and plaster forerunner to the Brighton Pavilion.

Before leaving the soil of the original Kew Gardens to cross the no longer extant Love Lane into Richmond Gardens, one more fantastical building deserves comment: the Gothic Cathedral. It stood more or less to your right, where Burton's Temperate House now pompously stands. The cathedral was a fragile structure

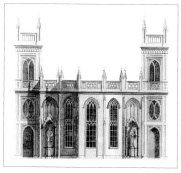

of wood and plaster built in 1759 and demolished in 1807. It was designed by a Swiss, Johann Heinrich Müntz, who had been a protegé of Horace Walpole upstream until thrown out of the house for an affair with one of his servants. Its importance lies in the fashion, alongside classical and oriental works, for gothic follies. Fortunate landowners already had crumbling ruins on their estate.

Cross the first tarmac path (which roughly follows the line where Love Lane once ran); **cross the second tarmac path but turn left along the third (you'll find a signpost for Queen Charlotte's Cottage at the path crossing).** As you walk you will pass through a short larch avenue. Larches are peculiar among conifers for being deciduous. Britain is the improbable location of two specific varieties, a hybrid between the European and Japanese larch which arose by chance at Blair Atholl around 1900. Being taller than either parent it became the firm favourite for commercial forestry. The other, probably a unique sport, is the 'creeping larch,' a prostrate variety of the European larch, at Henham Hall, Suffolk. Only 2.5 metres high, it has a 26 metre spread.

Follow the tarmac path until you reach Queen Charlotte's cottage.

Queen Charlotte's cottage is more than a sweet-looking edifice. Charlotte may have designed it herself. Built c.1770, it faced onto an oval paddock, about three acres in size, all surrounded by woodland. Around the paddock were sixteen animal pens, housing an array of exotic birds and beasts: pheasant, North African and Indian cattle, a 'hog like a porcupine in skin, with navel on back' and the acme of this menagerie, a pen of kangaroos. Menageries were a fashionable royal appurtenance. James I had had one 150 years earlier in St James' Park, so had Queen Caroline in Richmond Gardens in the 1730s, composed of 'deer and wild beasts,' which apparently included tigers. It was the appeal of the exotic. As for the cottage itself, one might describe it as *faux*-rustic, in fact, a *cottage orné*. It conformed to the growing fashion of the aristocracy to delight in a fantasy of Arcadia, a picturesque peasant life, one might say, minus the sweat, the poverty or the midden. At the same time, however, an increasing number of the gentry class were taking a much more serious interest in farming, getting their hands dirty, building model farms, experimenting with livestock breeding, for example George III himself, and thinking through every aspect of high yield agriculture. In this Britain was a world leader.

Resume the path (now without tarmac) and follow it without deviation until you reach a T-junction with a small drinking fountain. Turn left and follow the path around to the right and find a seat facing Syon House across the river.

Capability Brown's changes to the appearance of Syon House grounds on the Middlesex bank are described on p.54. Brown is a good deal less popular on the Surrey bank, where he permanently changed the formal landscape of Richmond Gardens.

Ormonde had built a short terrace along the riverbank facing Syon in 1714. Caroline decided to make something more dramatic out of his efforts. Ormonde's terrace began at the bend in the river 200 metres upstream from where you are standing (see Griffier's depiction, p.54). What he began, Caroline finished in 1729-34. The Great Terrace ran for about half a mile towards Kew. It was backed by a row of elms. This grassy terrace soon attracted fashionable crowds. Brown's crime in 1765, in league with Caroline's grandson George III, was to destroy this great edifice in order to bring the garden landscape 'naturally' right down to the river.

In so doing, Brown destroyed a rare early eighteenth century garden feature. In any case, the garden still had to be separated from the river by a ha-ha (Walk No. 2, p.52) and a decade later a towpath was laid on the outer perimeter of the estate, thus vitiating the intended 'natural' foreshore.

Turn around. Before walking back along the Syon Vista in the direction of the Palm House, pause.

If in season and if still cultivated, admire the cornfield in front of you. It has been planted with the wild flowers of arable land from Kew's seed bank at Wakehurst Place. With chemical farming most of these species have now largely disappeared from the countryside. Do we want high-yield crops or bio-diversity? We may still not understand the true price we are paying for non-organic farming.

As you walk towards the Palm House, find a seat as you pass the lake on your right.

Queen Caroline was obsessed by her garden and she solicited the assistance of the king's gardener, Charles Bridgeman, and also the artist and designer, William Kent. Both were at the forefront of the transition from formality to 'natural' landscape in the early eighteenth century. Both had worked closely with Alexander Pope at Twickenham, either developing ideas of gardening or putting these ideas into practice.

Much of the estate was still open field, so Caroline was free to fulfil her arcadian fantasies. She developed her 'Richmond Gardens' to the north of Richmond Lodge, leaving the ground to the south as a deer park. It is this landscape, which we know once existed here, that is so hard to recapture, since Brown and subsequent gardeners completely transformed it. But I shall try.

Imagine, for a moment, visitors walking through George and Caroline's grounds from Richmond. They would have passed Richmond Lodge, and a long formal canal, designed by Bridgeman in about 1728. To the right of the formal grounds running from the Lodge to the river, lay the wilderness, in the words of an admirer, a place of 'agreeable wildness and pleasing irregularity.' It started very approximately where Queen Charlotte's cottage now stands. This wilderness, too, was Bridgeman's creation. It was composed of labyrinthine walks of closely clipped hedges. Or one might

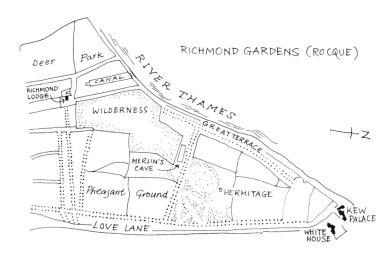

choose to walk to the riverfront, to promenade along the Great
Terrace that (now Queen) Caroline had extended and admire Syon
on the far bank.

Alternatively, one might
have turned inland through the
'forest'. Where the Azalea
Garden now lies, about 200m
away, once stood the
Hermitage, the first fantasy
structure Kent built for Queen
Caroline. Built in 1732, it

jutted out from a 10 metre high mound provided by Bridgeman.
'Very Gothic,' proclaimed *The Craftsman*, 'being a Heap of Stones
thrown into a very artful Disorder, and curiously embellished with
Moss and Shrubs' but the entrance was barred with 'costly gilt rails'
which showed 'an absurdity of taste.' In fact, while the idea was
clearly 'Gothick,' the building was decidedly classical, and
contained alcoves for busts of recent British worthies, for example
Robert Boyle (natural philosophy), Isaac Newton (natural

philosophy) and John Locke (political philosophy). The Hermitage seems to have survived Brown's destruction of Caroline's garden, but became increasingly ruined and disappeared in the mid-nineteenth century.

Where the lake now lies, there was a large rectangular duck pond. At its south-eastern corner stood one of Kent's fantasy buildings. This was Merlin's Cave, built in 1735. Behind it, doubtless with spoil from the duck pond, reared a mount, on which  Bridgeman planted no fewer than 130 of his much loved elms. Merlin's cave was remarkable for a number of reasons. First, its three thatched 'beehive' roofs, were preposterous fantasies without historical precedent. Its entrance was a gothic ogee, and inside lay a central circular pavilion, resting on four wooden pillars, flanked by octagonal chambers. A gothic apse allowed for three waxworks made by Mrs Salmon of Fleet Street, who specialised in the horrific, the comical and the grotesque. Her Fleet Street establishment included the execution of Charles I, and the child-sacrifice Rites of Moloch. Pride of place, however, was ceded to a decidedly medical tableau: 'Margaret, Countess of Heningbergh, Lying on a Bed of State, with her Three Hundred and Sixty-Five Children, all born at one birth.' Attendance could become addictive. William Hogarth confessed to having 'frequently loitered at Old Mother Salmon's.'

By contrast, the waxworks in Merlin's Cave seem to have been sadly uninspiring and the cave did not enjoy the approbation of the Hermitage. Horace Walpole mocked it as 'an unintelligible puppet show'. Caroline, hurt by such sniping, sought her husband's sympathy. But in vain, for George responded, 'I am very glad of it... you deserve to be abused for such childish silly stuff.' The Cave was also equipped with a real peasant poet, Stephen Duck, a labourer's son from the Vale of Pewsey. Duck went on to take an appointment in the Yeomen of the Guard; to become keeper of Duck Island in St James' Park and to take holy orders before drowning himself, apparently in a fit of dejection, in 1756. Ten years later Brown demolished Merlin's Cave, along with the Great Terrace and the Wilderness with its woodland walks.

And what of Brown's work here? Nothing remains except the Rhododendron Dell, and the perimeter ha-ha. The present landscaped lake was dug under the direction of one of Kew's great directors, William Hooker, and filled by the tidal Thames in 1861.

Continue walking along the vista towards the Palm House. Syon Vista was first planted with alternating limes and deodar cedars in 1851. Twenty years later it was embellished with Douglas firs and evergreen oaks. Only evergreen oaks and a few limes survive. The deodars and firs must have skulked off. Half way along, down near the lakeside you may notice an enormous pollarded English oak, which must predate even Ormonde, and be part of the agricultural landscape before any gardens were here. It may have been a hedgerow tree.

Once across the tarmac path look out on your right for the enormous and magnificent Lucombe oak. This oak was first raised by chance by an Exeter nurseryman, William Lucombe about 1762. It is a hybrid between the cork oak and the Turkey oak. Lucombe noticed how much more vigorous it was than his other seedlings, growing seven metres in seven years, an astonishing feat for an oak. This particular specimen cannot, surely, be older than 1830, since it was moved in 1846 to make way for the proposed Syon vista.

On reaching the Rose Garden ascend the steps of the Palm House, and with your back to its door, turn around.

This is as good a place as any to get a brief idea of the way the developments of the nineteenth century largely erased the previous phases of the two eighteenth century formal and landscaped gardens. With the proposed creation of the Palm House, Kew Gardens was again torn between serious botanical work and the idea of 'pleasure gardens'. That tension is apparent here. While the Palm House was being planned, a water colourist-turned-landscape architect, William Nesfield, played the principal role in designing the look of the gardens radiating from this new focal point to the Gardens. Nesfield was enamoured of the *parterres* and *pattes d'oie* ('goose foot') vistas, harking back to the highly formalised garden layout of late seventeenth century princely gardens. He sought to create a Victorian version. What is left of his *parterre* stands before you as a Rose Garden. With regard to the *patte d'oie*, the left vista runs to the Pagoda, lined with cypress, scarlet thorn and juniper, backed by deodar cedars. The central Syon Vista, now a green-sward, was laid with a substantial gravel walk leading to a proposed obelisk on the riverbank. Finally, on the right, the third vista of the intended *patte d'oie* runs only a few yards to a venerable Cedar of Lebanon. Hooker made sure Nesfield's passion for clipped shrubs and neat geometric flowerbeds was kept under strict control. In fact the *parterre* never really succeeded. The ground here is a frost pocket, so bad that bricks have been laid under the earth to ensure good drainage and to keep the earth warmer. Even so, only hardy roses grow here now.

Free at last, you are dismissed, to roam.

RECOMMENDED CHOICES, on the Garden Map:

Indoors:

Each of the **glass houses** has its own delights on offer.

The Plants and People Museum, facing across the pond to the Palm House.

The Evolution House behind the Temperate House.

The Marianne North Gallery.

Outdoors:

The Order Beds, beyond the Princess of Wales Conservatory, first established in 1846 on George III's old vegetable garden, set out the different plant species according to genus. Almost all the seeds used here have been gathered from wild plants. It is well labelled for anyone interested in horticulture or botany.

The Rock Garden, beyond the Order Beds, was first created in 1882, intended to represent a typical Pyrenees watercourse. In 1929 it was rebuilt using, as one can see, a massive quantity of Sussex sandstone.

The Bamboo Garden and **Minka House** are both close to the Rhododendron Dell.

4 *Kew Bridge to Barnes on the Middlesex Bank, and back via Mortlake*

Distance 7 km: 2.5 hours

WARNING: At high water sections of path on both banks can be completely inundated, following which even at low water the path can remain very muddy.

This walk takes you downstream along the Middlesex Bank to Barnes Bridge and back along the Surrey Bank to Kew.

Start from the Surrey bank of Kew Bridge, downstream side.

As you walk up the ramp of the bridge, look over the side. Tacked onto the last building on your right, facing the Memorial Garden, is a tiny mortuary once used as a temporary resting place for bodies washed up along this stretch of river, at one time a not uncommon occurrence.

The present bridge is the third to be built. The first was completed in 1759. Seven of its eleven arches were made of timber, and the central span was 50 feet in width, to accommodate river traffic. It soon proved shaky, sufficiently so that Horace Walpole and a friend, Lady Browne, returning from a dinner party one night, rashly opted to take the horse-ferry at Richmond:

> 'We embarked and had five men to push the ferry. The night was very dark, for though the moon was up we could neither see her, nor she us. The bargemen were drunk, the poles would scarce reach the bottom, and in five minutes the rapidity of the current turned the barge round, and in an

instant we were at Isleworth. The drunkenest of the men called out, "She is gone, she is lost!" meaning they had lost the management. Lady Browne fell into an agony, began screaming and praying to Jesus and every land and water goddess, and I, who expected not to stop till we should run against Kew Bridge, was contriving how we should get home; or what was worse, whether I must not step into some mud up to my middle, be wet through, and get the gout. With much ado they recovered the barge and turned it; but then we ran against the piles of the new bridge, which started the horses, who began kicking.'

In 1773, after barely 13 years' use, the bridge was closed. A new bridge made of stone was started in 1782 and completed in 1789. The present bridge was built in 1903.

If it is a cold day, be grateful it is not so cold as late November 1788, when a sheep was roasted whole on the ice, just downstream of the bridge.

Cross to the Middlesex bank on the downstream side of the bridge and turn right, downstream.

It is a nice thought that when the railway cutting was dug in 1838, 100 metres to the north of the bridge, mammoth, rhinoceros, aurochs and hippopotamus bones were found sandwiched between the London clay and the river gravel, being therefore over 500,000 years old.

Cleave to the riverbank along Strand-on-the-Green.

The long building on the left of the road, 'Pier House', was originally a laundry. The café on the corner was, as one can tell, once a pub, *The Steam Packet*.

Just before the riverfront parts company from the carriageway,

Malthouse, c. 1900.

you may care to note No. 84, Rose Cottage, where Nancy Mitford lived during the Second World War and where she wrote *The Pursuit of Love*.

Make for the path in front of the row of houses facing directly onto the river.

The very first of the houses on the riverbank is modern and replaced a malthouse, demolished in 1925. In the late nineteenth century there were no fewer than five malthouses along Strand-on-the-Green. If you are wondering why, it is because the fields of Chiswick and Fulham produced outstandingly good barley. Malting along this riverbank has a long history. People were producing malt in Chiswick in the early thirteenth century, if not earlier. Production here only stopped in the twentieth century. Placed on the riverbank, the malthouses could consign their malt (and also raw barley) easily

'Bommer' Pearce, probably the last fisherman of the Pearce family. By the time this photograph was taken, c.1880, there was precious little fishing to be had and his peterboat (see p.234) has been adapted (the addition of crude wooden fixed-pin rowlocks) as a 'bumboat' for carrying goods, hence his alleged nickname 'Bommer'.

by barge. (On the mysteries of malting and beer brewing, see p.260.)

Fishing was the principal rationale of Strand-on-the-Green, from the early middle ages, if not earlier, until the nineteenth century (for more on fishing, etc., see p.224). The most notable fisher dynasty here was the family Pearce, the last to hold a royal grant to fish with nets and eel pots. The family was immortalised through its connection with the painter Zoffany (see below).

Until c.1760 Strand-on-the Green was composed largely of cottages for fishermen, bargemen, boatbuilders and maltsters. Then more gentry houses started to appear, not least because of the construction of Kew Bridge and the growth of the royal court at Kew. But by 1900 Strand-on-the-Green was so impoverished it was almost a slum.

A FEW NOTES ON HOUSES OF INTEREST:

No. 70, Zachary House, is supposedly named after a mariner shipwrecked in the West Indies who proceeded to swim '22 leagues' to another island. Forget the swimming: the early rubbed brickwork around the porch is worth more than a glance.

No. 69 was once home to Marshal of the Royal Air Force Sir John Slessor. Slessor became a leading advocate of bombing 'industrial workers, whose morale and sticking power cannot be expected to equal that of disciplined soldiers,' as he put it. Like others, he was proved wrong. Warplanes on both sides laid waste towns and cities, causing thousands of civilian casualties but failing to break the will of the civil population. He was, one imagines, possibly the only resident to feel entirely at home under the Heathrow flight path.

No 66 Springfield House, the pick of gentry houses together with No. 65, both date from c. 1700. No. 65 was home to Johann Zoffany (1733-1810), who came to Britain in 1758 and spent the last 20 years of his life here. He kept a boat for parties on the Thames: 'a decked sailing-vessel, elegantly and conveniently fitted up, on board of which we frequently went... while servants were put into a magnificent livery of scarlet and gold with blue facings....' Zoffany also built a summerhouse in a tree overhanging the river here, to allow a harpsichordist and harpists to play within earshot of the Prince of Wales on the royal barge.

When Zoffany painted a depiction of the *Last Supper* for St Anne's, Kew, it was to his neighbours, the family Pearce, that he turned to model for it. Judas Iscariot, however, apparently bore an uncanny resemblance not to one of the family Pearce but to a lawyer at St Anne's with whom Zoffany had fallen out over the drafting of his will. One suspects Zoffany felt he had been swindled. A row ensued. Zoffany refused to alter the offending face. So St Anne's rejected the painting and it eventually ended up in St Paul's, Brentford. So if you wish to know what the Pearce clan looked like *circa* 1790, make a minor detour on Walk No 2. You will be thinking Zoffany would not have darkened the door of St Anne's again. In fact he was buried there in 1810, so there may have been a sneaking sympathy at St Anne's with his portrayal.

Look out for Oliver's Ait. This ait was purchased by the Thames Conservancy when it built the Surrey towpath and was:

> 'ornamented with a wooden building, in the form of a castle….. fitted up as an habitation for those persons who are appointed to receive the tolls which the city of London is empowered to collect from trading barges, according to their tonnage, to pay the interest of the loan raised to improve the navigation of this part of the river.'

Back to the houses:

No. 56, Ship House Cottage: Dylan Thomas sometimes slept here.

Nos 55-52 are rather grand for this riverfront, and faced with white Suffolk brick, a very up-market class of brick at the time.

No. 47 is an old malt house.

Nos. 43-40 demonstrate that thoroughly modern buildings can be highly successful in a row of old ones.

The Moorings was built on the site of a derelict malt house in the 1930s. Ex-malthouses still stand on either side.

Magnolia Wharf is a more reticent 1960s development, replacing barge workshops. No 14 was home to Hugh Cudlipp (d. 1998), a press baron with only nine years' schooling to his name. Editor of the *Sunday Pictorial* at the age of 24, Cudlipp published Fleet Street's first topless model in 1938, 30 years before the *Sun*. He resorted to such tawdry measures to enlarge and engage his readership for the key issues of the day. He changed the tone of the paper from fainthearted acquiescence with fascism to strident condemnation. As Edward Hulton wrote of him in 1940:

'Cudlipp is just fed up with the evil complacency which is still the order of the day in this country.... His bursting impatience for genuine reform is almost irritating.'

Cudlipp lost none of his fire in old age. He was appalled by:

'the dawn of the Dark Ages of tabloid journalism, the decades still with us when the proprietors and editors – not all, but most – decided that playing a continuing role in public enlightenment was no longer any business of the popular press..... It was an age when investigative journalism in the public interest shed its integrity and became intrusive journalism for the prurient, when nothing, however personal, was any longer secret or sacred and the basic human right to privacy was banished in the interest of publishing profit....'

Just thought you might like to know.

Nos. 32-29 were rebuilt following war damage. Members of the Pearce family lived in the previous dwellings.

The *City Barge* pub was named in the nineteenth century after the Lord Mayor's Barge moored opposite (more on this on the Surrey bank). It was kept by another Pearce, Jack. Previously it was called *The Navigators' Arms*, the original building apparently of fifteenth century origin.

No. 23 is blatant concrete and glass, 1960s architecture at its best.

Pass under the rail-bridge, which was first opened in the 1868. Note the highly gothicised brick and stone pier, a forlorn attempt to deny the essential modernity of the industrial age.

The *Bull's Head Inn*, No 15. Oliver Cromwell's association with this pub is wholly fictitious.

Do not miss **the row of almshouses**, built in 1724 as six dwellings, now heavily restored as three still – by our standards – tiny dwellings. They give a good idea of the modest living quarters for most people at that time. The stone inset testifies to the charitable spirit of the donors.

No 1, rebuilt in 1788, is a delight with its central timber-cladded bay perched on Tuscan columns. Originally the bay was brickwork, the subsequent cladding was the idea of Edward Armitage, who designed the National Trust emblem, to suggest waterfront architecture.

When the footpath brings you back to the road, maintain the same direction along Grove Park Road.

Grove Park Road runs through the old Grove Park estate, developed in the second half of the nineteenth century. Look out on the right for handsome examples built in 1871. Nos. 74-68, in the words of Bridget Cherry, author of the current Pevsner, are 'a jolly

Maynard's boathouse, located where Strand-on-the-Green borders Grove Park. Maynard set up his business for city gents, before Grove Park became a suburb.

composition with turrets and crow stepped gables.' Built in 1874, they are the work of William Sargeant, a local man. He also built the best-known early electric boats. Having lived at No. 70, he moved to Zachary House on the Strand in 1888. The same year he collaborated with Immisch, who worked at Hampton (see vol. 1, p.24), to launch the largest electric-powered vessel ever.

There is a brief cul-de sac access to the riverbank just before the Redcliffe Gardens development.

It is regrettable the developers were not required to ensure public access *around* the perimeter of its essay in exclusivity, but one gets a great view from the access one is given and the chance to see the surviving façade of Thames Bank, a neo-Tudor mansion before demolition to construct the present residences. The Redcliffe Gardens itself seeks reassurance in a pastiche from the past, in a Wren style. All the gates are to keep Chiswick's brigands at bay.

Follow the right fork, Hartington Road. It is long and fortitude is advised.

On your left: St Paul's Church, 1872, was paid for by the Duke of Devonshire, who owned the Grove Park estate. Externally unremarkable it may seem, but go inside and you find that such suburban churches are often cherished centres of local community life, which also demonstrate practical passion about issues such as poverty, fair trade and social justice.

On your right stands Hartington Court, built in 1938 and confidently true to the style of that period.

No. 35 still has its original 1890s iron gates, surreptitiously extended to accommodate the internal combustion engine.

Chiswick Staithe, 1964, contains 69 dwellings. At its centre, facing the road, is a small 'mews' for garaging cars. Behind it lies a communal garden, an idea introduced from Sweden. All you probably wished to know was what a staithe might be. It is a virtually redundant word for a bank, a shore or an embankment.

Chiswick Quay was built in 1974, around a marina, itself originally a lake in Grove Park House gardens. Note the end houses with hung-tiles. Tile-hanging is a south-east style dating from the seventeenth century. Before houses had roof gutters and generous eaves, one can see how hung tiles might make a significant difference to the dryness of walls, particularly if these were wattle and daub.

During the First World War, long before Chiswick Quay was thought of, concrete barges were built here for transporting munitions to France.

On your left, just before the sports buildings you may notice three old sweet chestnut trees, the last ghosts of the substantial number of chestnut and walnut trees that stood in the Grove House estate. A little further on, the Polytechnic Grandstand dates from 1936 (by Joseph Addison). The sports ground was purchased for the Polytechnic of Central London, now the University of Westminster.

At the end of Hartington Road, cross the main road when traffic allows, and follow the road back down to the riverbank.

Chiswick Bridge was built at the same time as Twickenham Bridge, for the same purpose, namely the new carriageway to Chertsey, and was opened in 1933. The engineer for both bridges was Alfred Dryland. However, the architect here was Sir Herbert Baker, who had made his name in the late nineteenth century by his collaboration with Rhodes in creating Groote Schuur in the Dutch colonial style as the South African prime minister's residence. Baker was only ten years Ayrton's senior, but he was almost 70 when he worked on Chiswick Bridge and perhaps this shows in the treatment. Where at Twickenham Ayrton frankly proclaimed his building material, Baker clothed the rude ferro-concrete structure at Chiswick in beguiling Portland stone, 3,400 tons of it.

Follow the path along the riverbank (to Barnes rail bridge).

Almost immediately you will pass the Boat Race finishing post, striped in dark and light blue. It will be a while before you see it again from the Surrey bank.

The land here, Duke's Meadows, has always been too marshy for building, hence the golf club and the delightful allotments. But do not think for one moment that the ground has been left undisturbed. In 1924 Duke's Meadows was given over to gravel extraction by Concrete Aggregates Ltd, a sister company of the Ham River Grit Company (see p.155 and also vol. 1, p.136). Tests showed the gravel to be of very high quality. Virtually the whole area was excavated in

Gravel extraction, Duke's Meadows.

Tom Green's boathouse, now the site of a nature reserve.

just over 13 years. Two million cubic yards of aggregate and sand were extracted, an almost unimaginable quantity, all from one hole, so to speak. After the initial two years of extraction, the company progressively refilled, presumably with builders' rubble.

Another longish walk along the river bank (but be grateful for a break in my commentary). When you reach the Chiswick boathouse you will be compelled to follow the road to the left.

Take heart from the fact that your detour is partly to protect a small nature reserve nestling around a stream inlet close to the railway embankment and the river. A boathouse once stood here, belonging to a famous waterman, Tom Green, who had won Doggett's coat and badge in 1872 (see p.238). He coached some of the finest scullers of his day. In 1886 he coached an Australian blacksmith, Bill Beach, for the world championship on the Putney-Mortlake course against an American, Jack Gaudaur. During the race, Green waited at his boathouse. Gaudaur came into view first. Beach was clearly exhausted. The race appeared over. Green shouted to Beach to stop and pull in to the bank. It was an unprecedented instruction in a race. He splashed Beach's face with water and said, 'Now, Bill, think of your wife and children, and go after him for he's as bad as you!' Beach won on the finishing post. So great was his own mental stress that Green was taken ill at the finish. Beach, physically exhausted but emotionally triumphant, sat by his bedside all night.

Continue to follow the road under the bridge and turn right back towards the riverbank, cleaving to the right to follow the footpath alongside the railway embankment. Turn right at the end and cross Barnes Bridge, pausing to enjoy the view.

Barnes Bridge was originally built for the single track loop line from Barnes to Hounslow via Chiswick. Designed by Joseph Locke (see p.23), it was widened in 1891 with the wrought iron arches ('bowstring trusses' to the *cognoscenti*) added. They were doubtless an engineering triumph but equally doubtless something of a visual disaster.

Descend from the bridge and immediately cross to the riverbank and turn upstream along the towpath under the bridge.

Under the bridge you have a chance to admire the single-track elegance of Locke's original structure.

Immediately on your left, look out for The Tower, Elm Bank Gardens, with its tower, decorated in mock Venetian gothic, proof that your most secret building fantasies can indeed be fulfilled. The tower stood in the grounds of Elm Bank House, an eighteenth century mansion, demolished in 1904. The decorative urns on the wall are from the old east gateway to the house.

As you pass the lime trees on your left, sit down and steel yourself for a real shocker.

On 21 January 1907 a London General motor omnibus left the road here. Under the banner 'Amazing Scenes: Passengers' Perilous Plight', *The Daily News* tells the tale far better than I:

> 'The bus was running the usual route from Liverpool-st. to Barnes at about half past seven last night… Anyway, the bus – which was being driven on the third speed just here (as is always the case) – suddenly swerved to the right and ran amok. It dashed into the heavy wooden railings and shattered them like matchstick. Then with a drunken heave it crashed down the steep stone-paved bank, plump into the river. There were a lot of people about at the time. Women on the pavement shrieked and fainted with terror, as the monster vehicle lurched into the stream, apparently carrying its crew to certain death.
>
> The remaining passengers on the bus were sitting upstairs on one of the back seats. They were a young man and his sweetheart, out for the afternoon – their names Henry Amos of Ruskin-buildings, Westminster and Jenny Saunderson, of Trinity Mews, Pimlico.
>
> As the bus charged the railings they both started up – the girl screaming with fright. She clung to Amos, but he was flung like a stone from a catapult right to the further end of the omnibus, where he fell and injured his leg. The next moment the bus was in the river. The driver, Fred Searle, clung manfully to his wheel, and had the brakes jammed on hard as the cumbersome vehicle struck the water.
>
> Down she went, and before Searle could realise what had happened the water was over his shoulders and dashing into his face. He was up to his neck, when the fore part of the bus grounded in the mud, the machinery whirred madly, and then

stood still. By some miracle the vehicle kept upright, and in that position came to a standstill.'

Searle was fished out of the water by boat, while Amos and his girlfriend limped home, perhaps more distressed by so public a disclosure of their courtship than by the bruises they had sustained.

BUILDINGS OF PASSING INTEREST:

If you enjoy football, watch out for **No 26**, The Terrace (c.1720), for this supposedly is where the Football Association was founded in 1863.

No. 27 is the scene of yet another shock, which took place in July 1812. The French political émigré couple living here, the Count and Countess d'Antraigues, were stabbed to death by their Italian manservant, Lorenzo, who then rushed upstairs and blew his own brains out. No motive was ever established. That's Latin passion for you. Lorenzo was promptly buried on the edge of Barnes Common. However, five days later a complaint appeared later in the columns of *The Times* that Lorenzo's grave had been repeatedly opened to allow people to gawp. Furthermore,

> 'The indecency was aggravated by the hearses containing the unhappy Count and Countess d'Antraigues, after a brisk trot across the common, drawing up by the assassin's grave, where the attendants satiated themselves with a deliberate view of the body. Two stagecoaches accompanied by a crowd of horsemen, women and children, contemplated this disgusting scene for twenty minutes.'

And that's British prurience for you.

No 31 was built *circa* 1720.

Nos. 32 and 33 are early Victorian semis, heralding the beginning of suburbia. The generous windows are characteristic more of the Regency era.

On entering the purlieus of Mortlake it is as well to master your nomenclature, just in case you are challenged. Forget all the myths about plague burials, and stagnant water. 'Mort' probably refers to a local Saxon strongman, possibly called Morta. The 'lake' ending, *lacu*, does indeed indicate water but more probably a stream that debouched into the Thames somewhere along here, or possibly Beverley Brook which runs across the south side of Mortlake and Barnes before reaching the Thames. It could also be handy to arm yourself with another little known fact. In the last years of the eighteenth century no less than 60 acres of Mortlake's arable land was, like much of this stretch of the Surrey bank, devoted to the cultivation of asparagus, by 1800 a crop nearly tenfold as profitable per acre as wheat. Before concluding, however, that Mortlake's citizenry was thus rendered distinctive by the odour of their pee, one should be aware that the asparagus was all for export to the City. Asparagus had been introduced to England as a novelty in the sixteenth century and was popularly known as 'sparrowgrass'. In 1832 the Duchess of Bedford was presented with a bundle of asparagus weighing 15kg, by the leading asparagus cultivator of the parish. She must have had strong arms.

As you pass the rear of Mortlake High Street buildings you may care to note:

The *White Hart* pub: in the 1840s it was possible to catch a paddle steamer here for Margate. Margate? It was a principal summer seaside resort for London's middle classes, *pater familias* joining the rest of the family at week-ends.

Tideway Wharf, converted into flats in 1989 and the Yard a couple of years later.

The Old Fire Station, 1904, London stocks with red brick around the windows, was refurbished in 2000 as architectural offices.

No 123, the Limes, c.1720, with its handsome pillared porch facing the river, was home to the philanthropist, Quintin Hogg. Hogg was the driving force behind the polytechnic movement, following his purchase of the Royal Polytechnic Institution in 1882, which he opened for athletic, intellectual, spiritual and social recreation. The evidence may be seen on the way upstream. In 1895 the Limes became the new council office after the compulsory marriage between Barnes and Mortlake, its unenthusiastic spouse, in 1893. The building took a hit during the Second World War.

You may be thinking this great curving sweep of the Thames was a wonderful spot for the weekend 'cottage' which the great and the good of eighteenth century London were so keen on having. But remember the pong or, rather, pongs. Dung barges made their way upstream here to provide farmland dressing for the farms and market gardens that fed the city. One immediately thinks of the compelling demands of that asparagus. Meanwhile, onshore, the Mortlake pottery belched forth toxic fumes from the salt glaze used during firing. A pottery had been established in 1743 about 300 metres upstream, and a second on the opposite site of Mortlake High Street around 1800. To cap it all, the brewery even further upstream and upwind, emitted the warm and foetid vapours of brewing. You needed strong nostrils to live in Mortlake.

Watch out for the granite setts on the ground, angled to give grip to horses' hooves.

Smelly, Mortlake may have been. Yet if you were here in 1901 you smugly knew that the old Power Station on your left, now office accommodation, and the electricity substation, still operative, produced the cheapest power in the realm.

Straight after, Jubilee Gardens are the remains of the garden of

The Limes, marred now by the harshness of the concrete floodwall.

Immediately next to Jubilee Gardens stands a small building attached to a larger more handsome one on its right. This is Suthrey House, also known as the Upper Dutch House, the only surviving part of the Mortlake Tapestry Works, established in 1619. The location combined good river communications with extreme dampness, an essential requirement to relax tension on the warp, and also cheapness compared with the higher land prices closer to the City. The premises extended for about 100 metres upstream. The other principal building, the Lower Dutch House, fell derelict and was finally demolished in 1950. The business was initially a wild success, thanks mainly to the patronage of Charles I, as Prince of Wales. He commissioned a considerable amount of work, most notably tapestries based on Raphael cartoons entitled *The Acts of the Apostles*, originally intended for tapestries in the Sistine Chapel. Thanks to the recruitment of Flemish master weavers, Mortlake produced tapestries that could match those of any factory in Paris or Flanders. Civil war put an end to royal commissions and, following the Restoration of 1662, Charles II proved more interested in painting. The factory never recovered, and finally closed in 1703.

Suthrey House was home to that late nineteenth century anti-imperialist and champion of the oppressed, Wilfrid Scawen Blunt. Blunt courted unpopularity by opposing the British occupation of Egypt in 1882 and supporting Home Rule for Ireland. It was to Blunt that his friend Muhammad Abduh, the great Egyptian religious reformer, wrote in 1884, asking him to tell the British: 'Do not attempt to do us any more good. Your good has done us too much harm already,' words that have proved tragically prescient of much greater and continuing destructive interference by the 'we-know-best' Western powers in the Muslim Arab world since then.

The site of the old tapestry works now contains a variety of delightful but run-down eighteenth century houses, in particular the

one with bow rear, complete with canopied balcony, facing onto the
river and commanding views both up and down stream.

**Watch out for the steps on your left and a glimpse of the
church tower. There's a handy pedestrian crossing if you
wish to inspect the church and grounds.**

The alley passes 'Tapestry Green', the site of the demolished Lower
Dutch House of the tapestry works. Since St Mary's Church is in all
probability locked, it may not be worth making a detour. The stone
tower dates from 1543, the year the church was moved, almost
certainly by order of Henry VIII, from its original site by the manor
house further upstream. The lower tower is typical of the fifteenth
century, the result of recycling of materials of that period. The rest of
the church is mostly the work of Arthur Blomfield, a distinguished
architect of the later nineteenth century. Round the back, the graveyard has been elegantly landscaped as a public space (perfect, if
you are carrying sandwiches). Somewhere below the chancel floor
supposedly lies Mortlake's most celebrated resident, John Dee
(1527-1608). As a scientist, geographer and mathematician, Dee
was unrivalled in England at that time. In John Aubrey's words:
'Hee had a very faire clear rosie complexion; a long beard as white
as milke; he was tall and slender....' Dee came to Mortlake in 1566
and lived almost opposite the new church, facing the river. Aubrey
liked eyewitness accounts:

> 'Old Goodwife Faldo (a Natif of Mortlak in Surrey) did
> know Dr Dee, and told me he did entertain the Polonian
> Ambassador at his howse in Mortlak, and dyed not long
> after; and that he shewed the Eclipse with a darke Roome to
> the said Ambassador. She beleeves he was eightie years old
> when he dyed. She sayd, he kept a great many Stilles goeing.
> That he layd the storme. That the Children dreaded him

Mortlake, c. 1900. The wooden steps lead into the Queen's Head *pub, while the nearer stone steps lead up to St Mary's Church. The barges appear to be laden with coal for local consumption.*

because he was accounted a Conjurer. He recovered the basket of Cloathes stollen, when she and his daughter (both Girles) were negligent; she knew this.'

It was his reputation for sorcery that got him into trouble. When he left his house to go abroad in 1583, a mob of locals broke in, destroying his furniture, his astronomy instruments and most of his huge library of an estimated 4,000 books and manuscripts.

St Mary's has a Vestry House attached, built in the 1660s. On completion it was sensibly put to use as a village school.

Resume walking along the riverbank.

At the foot of the same steps stands the *Queen's Head* pub, as was. Originally built in the eighteenth century it was rebuilt at the end of the nineteenth, and finally closed in 1932, to be turned into flats. Beyond it lie a variety of modern apartment blocks. One of these stands on the site of the Mortlake pottery.

An evocative view of Mortlake brewery. Bull's Alley is on the left (W. Luker, 1893).

Immediately after these apartment blocks, on your left, is the Mortlake drawdock, also known as Bull's Alley, probably in exactly the same location ever since the Middle Ages. This is where the manorial produce was loaded onto barges and where essential supplies from beyond the manor, including all that night soil, were unloaded.

Look out for the old crane rails running out onto the towpath. They mark the site of the old jib crane used for loading and unloading for the brewery.

The brewery itself stands on the site of the old manor house. This area was the heart of medieval Mortlake, where the old wharf was sited. The manor also included Wimbledon and Putney and belonged to the archbishops of Canterbury. Given the proximity of the royal palace at Sheen/Richmond, one can assume that Mortlake's importance from the mid-fourteenth century till the

View through the legs of the hydraulic crane at Mortlake Brewery wharf, probably late 1920s.

Civil War in the 1640s was less to do with its economic potential than its location. Archbishops needed ready access to the ear of the sovereign. No fewer than nine archbishops died here. By the time of the Reformation, the manor house probably resembled Knole, in Kent. Knole was built largely by Archbishop Bourchier, so in all probability it was he who built here. Having been appointed archbishop by the Lancastrians in 1454, Bourchier managed to forge a fruitful relationship with the House of York also. Finally, following the final defeat of the Yorkists in 1485, Bourchier married the Tudor Henry VII to Elizabeth of York in 1486. He never, it seems, put a word or foot out of place and Mortlake acquired immense importance in his time. Apart from the gatehouse, which went later, the palace buildings seem to have been destroyed around 1700, by which time they were already in a ruinous state.

The present brewery site grew during the nineteenth century, first with the introduction of steam power in 1840 and then with the advent of the big breweries, Watneys in 1899, followed by Budweiser in 1986, a firm that makes sure that anyone on the river is aware of its presence. At the end of the western end of the brewery stands the Granary Building, 1903. Tall and massive, it was originally the brewery's maltings, a monument to the working Thames. Empty since 1954, it lours over the river, its lower windows darkly shuttered.

Cross Ship Lane.

The Ship pub, originally the *Harteshorn* and later the *Blew Anchor*, dates back to Tudor times and possibly earlier.

Thames Cottage is eighteenth century, notable for its tall tile roof.

Tudor Lodge, c.1750. The front, consisting of six rooms, is original. The rear is early nineteenth century.

Thames Bank House, c.1730. The oldest part is at the rear. The canopied balcony is Regency.

Leyden House is the oldest house surviving in Mortlake. The rear part contains a late fifteenth century timber frame construction, encased in brick probably in the eighteenth century. A Tudor fireplace and chimney survive inside the building.

Parliament Mews and **Varsity Row** are impostors, of recent origin.

Look across the river to the Boat Race finishing post, painted in dark and light blue livery. There are few sporting events in which the disproportion between effort and outcome is so great, but you may like to know the origin of the finishing post. In 1877 there was a dead heat. It seems that Oxford probably won; Cambridge seems to have thought so. According to one, not impartial, Oxford eye-witness:

'The only person who had not seen it [the finish] was the umpire, old John Phelps, who had never seen a near race

before, and lost his head, and shut his eyes, and merely
maintained that "He could not tell who had won." Therefore
the two Presidents decided it must be called a dead heat; and
though Cambridge chivalrously offered the victory to
Oxford, the latter with still greater chivalry declined to
accept it.'

Punch wittily headlined its coverage: 'Oxford won, Cambridge
too'. Phelps was in his seventies with failing eyesight. To be fair to
him, there was no finishing post, an omission promptly rectified.
(For more on the Boat Race, see p.238)

Continue under the bridge.

Across the river, you may see the handsome Central London
Polytechnic (now Westminster University) and Ibis boathouses.
They were built in the 1880s, the former, at any rate, a tribute to
Hogg's philanthropy.

On your left stands the Mortlake Crematorium, built in 1939.
It is particularly remarkable for an unsung triumph of diplomacy,
for it was jointly financed by four boroughs, a political challenge
to make most borough finance officers quake. But it was the fact
that everything was electrically operated, even the death knell,
which caught attention at the time. It owes something to the legacy
of Edwin Lutyens in its use of brick and Portland stone. Serious
conflict broke out because the same access road was used by the
local borough for its refuse dump. It was far too near the knuckle
but somehow the borough got away with it. The offending dump
is discreetly hidden behind an earth mound, after Putney Town
Rowing Club boathouse.

We have entered the purlieus of East Sheen, originally probably
East *of* Sheen. At the end of the fifteenth century it was detached from
Mortlake to become a manor in its own right, the 300-acre manor of

East Sheen and West Hall. One of East Sheen's more famous sons, in reality a waterman's son, was John Partridge, apprenticed at a young age as a cordwainer in Covent Garden. The world of footwear was not enough, so he taught himself Latin, Greek, Hebrew, then physic, all in his free time. He was awarded the degree of Doctor of Physic at Leyden. He was appointed physician to Charles II but clearly this did not pay, and he was still making shoes in 1680 when he started publishing *Merlinus Liberatus*. So far, so good, a model Open University-style success, one might say. But *Merlinus Liberatus* was an almanac foretelling future events, for Partridge had taken up astrology too and this was to prove his undoing. Much of the favour his work enjoyed was on account of his Protestant fervour. Jonathan Swift decided to hoist him on his own predictions. Writing under a pseudonym Swift published a spoof almanac in 1708 which predicted that John Partridge 'will infallibly die upon 29 March next.' To complete the hoax Swift published a detailed account of his demise on 30 March. The jest once launched could not be retrieved. Until finally buried in Mortlake churchyard in 1715, Partridge vainly sought to persuade London he was still alive.

Watch out for five Lombardy poplars (if you wish to know more, see p.156) beside the development with mock regency balconies, Kew Riverside. This development stands on West Hall. Its lands stretched well into what was to become Richmond Park.

West Hall's land was largely arable inland but flood meadow and pasture closer to the river. The rapid growth of London from about 50,000 in 1500 to possibly 650,000 by 1700 vastly increased the demand for market garden produce for the city: asparagus, lettuce, peas, celery, rhubarb, radishes and liquorice. The soil along here is poor river gravel, but the heavy demand for fresh produce determined land use. There was an inlet just here where barges offloaded night soil from the city, used to fertilise the poor soil. Most of the riverside site became a large sewage works, c.1900, an irony that cannot have been lost on the last market gardeners (who finally packed up in 1938).

There was an enormous demand for fresh meat in the city also. These pastures and flood meadows were a last staging post on the drove road, before they were acquired for the sewage works. They were rented out to Welsh drovers for fattening up their livestock after the gruelling journey, before sale in the city.

Proceed, past the last vestige of the sewage works which, given a fair wind, will warn your nostrils of its presence.

Look out on the opposite bank for:

- A line of magnificent tall fir trees above the riverbank, just downstream of Hartington Court. These are the last remnant of the estate of Grove End House, a 'fantastic red-brick structure with tall capped towers' as an 1876 handbook described it. It had been built for a chamois leather merchant in 1861.
- Just above the distinctively 1930s Hartington Court apartments and almost opposite the National Archives, the elegant neo-Tudor riverfront of Thames Bank. Built in 1870 it was the second largest private residence in Chiswick. It once stood alone, before Redcliffe Gardens eviscerated and enclosed it with modern blocks either side.

Continue.

Half hidden by modern accommodation on your left, the National Archives, previously the Public Record Office, was first built on the site in 1977. To the President of the Kew Society it was 'an absolute monster'. Those that have used it, however, will be more forgiving. It is a wonderful treasure house, staffed by the most helpful curators one could ever ask for. The site had been orchards and market gardens until 1916 when the ground was requisitioned for a national insurance office. Various government buildings mouldered on the riverbank until the National Archives expanded over the whole site.

Just beyond is a small nature reserve. The notice tells all: double-lipped (Thames) door snails belong to a rare UK species, confined to a few locations along this stretch of the Thames. However, you will gaze through the railings in vain. If you are that double-lipped, you are bound to be shy.

Yet there is a much more serious tale to tell about this stretch of riverbank. Not so very long ago, fritillaries grew in the river meadows between Mortlake and Kew. Fritillaries have never been common, but they were well enough known in particular flood-meadow localities to acquire local names: 'leper's lily' in Somerset, 'shy widow' in Warwickshire, 'snake's head' in Oxfordshire. Sometimes they were simply named after the village near which they occurred. And this is the hard part to take: in 1860 the meadows along this riverbank were probably the *only* place in all Surrey where they still grew. There are only three or four places along the Thames or its tributaries where the fritillary has survived. If you wish to see them still darkly mysterious in their native habitat, go to the meadow behind Magdalen College, Oxford, in late April:

> 'And then I came to a field where the springing grass
> Was dulled by the hanging cups of fritillaries,
> Sullen and foreign-looking, the snaky flower,
> Scarfed in dull purple, like Egyptian girls
> Camping among the furze, staining the waste
> With foreign colour, sulky, dark and quaint....'
>
> Vita Sackville-West, *The Land*, 1926.

Continue under the railway bridge.

The allotments stand on Short Lotts, an area once apparently cultivated in strips by local peasant tenants before it was enclosed by Act of Parliament in 1823, a thought to please the aspirant peasants who cultivate it now. The enclosure act, 'to enclose part of Kew Green and dividing and extinguishing Rights of Common over certain lands...' put some plots of the meadows into local private hands hence, at the end of the allotments, the visible row (one of a pair) of cottages (Watcombe Cottages, 1887), sunk as it were behind the floodwall towpath. Just after them, the modern dwellings are built over a dock that was here in the eighteenth century and possibly earlier. The meadow on which these houses were built was known as 'Twiggets', probably a corruption of 'twig aits'. 'Twig' was an old local word for osiers, so one can imagine originally an ait, which then silted up to become part of the Surrey bank, as an osier bed or simply flood meadow.

The dock ran inland to Kew Green pond. By the nineteenth century the City of London Corporation kept its own ceremonial barge here, in a bespoke bargehouse on the bank. The building now standing on the City bargehouse site goes by the name of Toll House Studio. The following white building is the old City tollhouse. The present house was built in 1872 for the collector after he had complained that the tide rose within two feet of his sitting-room, enough to render the calmest of us anxious.

At the first opportunity turn left down steps and along the alley.

Thetis Terrace cottages are named after the mother of Achilles who, being a sea goddess, was fond of the damp and clearly should have been given the toll collector's old house. The Head Gardener of the Botanical Gardens, W.T. Aiton, did particularly well out of the enclosure act. All the cottages, from Watcombe Cottages to Thetis Terrace, were built on his award of land.

On your right lies the only part of the old meadow, Westerly Ware, that still remains open ground, albeit as a recreation ground and memorial garden. Westerley Ware ran upstream as far as Ferry Lane, 150 metres beyond the present Kew Bridge. Its name indicates that fishermen built weirs out into the river, zig-zag hurdles that trapped the fish. Long after the weirs had gone, nineteenth century pollution ended the fishing.

Turn left at the end of Thetis and Willow cottages and right at the end to emerge by Kew Green's pond.

The pond is probably medieval and may well have started life as a fishpond. With Westerly Ware (and implicitly an Easterly Ware a little downstream) fishing was clearly a principal economic activity. By the time of Henry VIII a channel had been cut from the river to allow the royal barge to dock here. In the nineteenth century carriages were washed here, as a ramp into the water indicates. The pond is still replenished by a sluice gate from the river.

Turn right.

The early twentieth century *Greyhound Inn* offers you some early photographs, including the original of the fisherman 'Bommer' Pearce, on its walls, and good food and drink from the bar.

Proceed towards the Bridge.

On your right just before the ramp stands a row of cottages, built in 1814 but named Waterloo Place in victorious celebration of that victory shortly after the building had been completed.

Chiswick House and Gardens

Distance 1 km: 1 hour (at least)

This walk provides a tour of the grounds of Chiswick House. It attempts to take you chronologically, as far as is reasonably possible, through the broad development of these gardens.

BEFORE YOU WALK

To get the most out of a visit there are a few essentials to understand beforehand, of which the most important is that the gardens were developed piecemeal but that, very crudely, one can usefully think in terms of the creation of three gardens, not one:

(1)   Burlington's original plot, on which he started work in 1716, was quite narrow, restricted on the west by the Bollo Brook, which runs into the Thames, and in the east by Moreton Hall (features R, S and T on sketch map overleaf).

(2)   The serpentine canal, known as the River (the Bollo Brook, as was), and the plots of land on the *west* side of it were acquired in 1726-27.

(3)   The estate of Moreton Hall, on the east side of Chiswick House, was acquired more than half a century after Burlington's death in 1753 by his heirs, the dukes of Devonshire. It was laid out in 1812 in a quite different fashion.

Burlington had acquired a Jacobean house at Chiswick on gaining his majority in 1715. He started his garden the following year, a full decade before he built his Palladian villa alongside the house. The garden of 1716-20 was laid along the axis of the avenue one can see

CHISWICK HOUSE AND GROUNDS

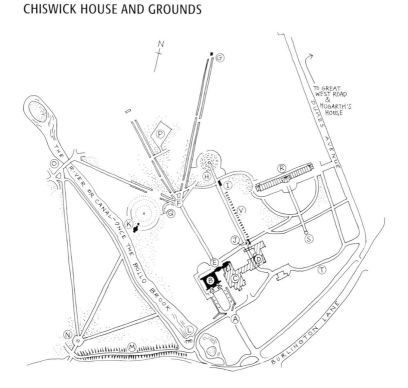

A   Principal Gate
B   The Villa
C   Site of Jacobean House
D   Site of Stables
E   Link Building
F   Heel of *Patte d'Oie*
G   Rustic Arch
H   Doric Column
I   Deer House
J   Inigo Jones Gateway
K   Ionic Temple & Orange Tree Garden

L   Cascade
M   Terrace
N   Obelisk
O   Bridge
P   Bowling Green
Q   Exedra
R   Conservatory
S   Sundial
T   Old Burlington Lane
V   Ha-Ha

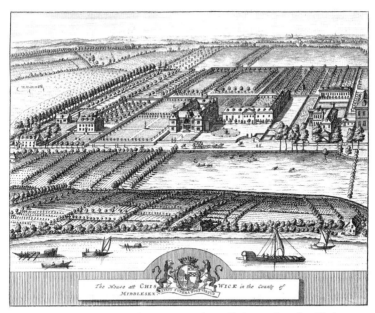

The Jacobean house at Chiswick, after Kip and Knyff, 1693. To the right of the house are the stables (demolished in the 1920s) and to the right of them stands Moreton Hall, acquired by the Devonshires in 1812 and demolished.

in Kip and Knyff's illustration, running along the left side of the Jacobean house into the distance, towards Gunnersbury.

Burlington never had a master plan for the garden he created. His work was piecemeal and, one might say, progressive. In part this reflected his growing understanding. He had spent 1714 on the Grand Tour and on his return he was assiduous in the study of architects like Andrea Palladio and Inigo Jones. Not satisfied, he went back to Italy in 1719 to deepen his understanding of Palladian architecture. This garden was his first effort in the classicism he had imbibed in Italy and is full of classical references, an attempt to imitate the gardens of 'Villas of the Ancients'. By 1720 Burlington, only 26 years old, was accepted in London as a leading if not *the* leading arbiter of cultural taste, later called by Horace Walpole the 'Apollo of the Arts.' Of course, he later repented of what he considered his first callow endeavours and asked his protégé, William Kent (see p.251), to help re-design parts of his original endeavours and to integrate them visually with the lands acquired in 1726, west of the Bollo Brook.

How does one have a master plan when the whole idea of the landscape garden is to work *with* the grain of nature? Burlington would have been familiar with the writing of his neighbour Alexander Pope:

> 'Those RULES of old discover'd, not devised,
> Are nature still, but Nature Methodiz'd…. '
>
> *An Essay on Criticism*, 1711.

Indeed, in 1731 Pope addressed Burlington directly, reinforcing his message: 'Consult the Genius of the Place in All' and ending with a promise:

> 'Nature shall join you, Time shall make it grow
> A Work to wonder at – perhaps a STOW.'
>
> *Epistle IV, To Richard Boyle, Earl of Burlington,* 1731

Stowe, of course, was where Kent had recently laid out a masterpiece. The message was clear. One must allow one's feelings on enhancing nature gently to mature and that means a gradualist approach.

The 'second' garden comprising the serpentine lake and all west of it was added in 1726-27 at the time work began on the Palladian villa. It is essentially the work of Kent. He took the departure from the formality of the seventeenth century (see p.247) a step further than Burlington: less symmetry, more winding paths, the Bollo Brook rendered a serpentine canal and vistas radiating from the new Burlington Lane gate in the south west corner of the garden. One can see this on Rocque's plan (see p.143).

Start at the entrance to the forecourt in the front of Chiswick House.

The entrance piers were once crowned with a pair of sphinxes, an unforgiving welcome to the classically informed. For in mythology the sphinx guarded the entrance to Thebes, devouring visitors unable to solve her riddle. The pair is now safely relocated in Green Park, a space bereft of riddles (but watch your back, there are three other sphinxes lurking behind the house). The main road ran past these gates, and was only re-routed further away from the house, in fact just on the flood plain, after Burlington's death. This explains the otherwise meaningless front area of the garden outside the entrance piers. Burlington laid an avenue of trees from his front gate, across the fields to the riverbank, providing a vista into the distance well beyond the road.

The forecourt is flanked with 'terms', carved heads on pedestals, backed by a yew hedge, installed during construction of the villa. Terms were boundary stones. Roman householders were encouraged on the feast of the god Terminus to honour their boundaries with their neighbours. It seemed right that the consequent boundary markers should represent Terminus himself.

Approach the house.

Burlington did not start building his villa, really a non-residential pavilion, until 1727. Yet it was the product of painstaking study of the work of principally Andrea Palladio and Inigo Jones but also of a student of Palladio, Vincenzo Scamozzi. Burlington worked out the design himself, as a result of the most careful study of his architectural mentors. One can see at a

PALLADIO'S VILLA ROTUNDA

SCAMOZZI'S
VILLA ROCCA DI PISANI

glance that the principal difference is Burlington's arrangement for the steps. Watch out for statues of Palladio and Jones to left and right of the steps respectively. Burlington liked publicly to acknowledge his mentors.

Walk around the left side of the house to the rear.

As you face the rear of the house, on your left stands the Link Building, added in 1733 to provide an indoor passage to the Jacobean house, which no longer exists. It was here that Burlington's wife, Dorothy Savile, took a lively interest in her husband's aesthetic endeavours in developing both the garden and the new villa.

Lady Burlington was, as they say, a character. Her chief claim to notoriety was on account of her volcanic rages. Lord Hervey, an eccentric from a highly eccentric family, summed her up:

'Let Dame Palladio, insolent and bold,

Like her own chairman, whistle, stamp and scold.'

Lord Chesterfield, present on an occasion when she had lost her favourite snuffbox, came away feeling cheated that she had not erupted as he had been led to expect. Even on her deathbed at Chiswick in 1758, she remained fearsome, in Walpole's words, 'the distemper shows itself oddly – she breaks out all over – in curses and blasphemies. Her maids are afraid of catching them and will hardly venture into her room.'

The Jacobean house, which had dominated the estate during Burlington's lifetime, was demolished in 1788 and two major wings added to the villa. It was here that a very much more attractive woman, Georgiana, the most celebrated of all duchesses of Devonshire, threw some of her glamorous parties. It is unlikely we could have resisted her charms, 'a lovely girl, natural, and full of grace', exclaimed Horace Walpole, 'the duchess of Devonshire effaces all

The two wings added to the villa in 1788.

without being a beauty; but her youth, figure, flowing good nature, sense, and lively modesty, and modest familiarity make her a phenomenon.' David Garrick went further (and so, chaps, you had better be sitting down): 'Exquisite, beautiful Young Creature. Were I five and twenty I could go mad about her, as I am past five and fifty I would only suffer martyrdom for her.' It is a real tribute to her qualities that she wowed the girls too. 'There is in her face, especially when she speaks,' wrote Fanny Burney, 'a sweetness of good humour and obligingness, that seem to be the natural and instinctive qualities of her disposition; joined to an openness of countenance that announces her endowed, by nature, with a character intended wholly for honesty, fairness and good purposes.' Too bad, she found herself married to a taciturn and emotionally frigid man, the 5th Duke.

The Link and the Summer Parlour, to the left of the villa and originally linking the Jacobean mansion, were both rescued from the regrettable demolition of the two Georgian wings in the 1950s. Their exteriors are restorations, but the interiors are original.

Turn around with your back to the Link Building.

You will immediately see how the garden's central axis is aligned on the Link Building, rather than on either the erstwhile Jacobean House or the Palladian villa, the real proof of how Burlington laid his garden out progressively, basing it on the avenue that was already there. Ignore for the moment, if you can, the lawns either side of the avenue leading into the distance. Burlington had inherited a walled enclosure, in fact a horse pasture, lined with trees and bisected by an avenue. It was separated from the old house by a knot garden, with parterres on the left side of the house (see illus. p.137). The avenue and walled pasture were off-centre from the Jacobean house and thus predated the idea propagated by Francis Bacon (see p.247) in 1597 that a house, its garden and the country beyond should enjoy visual integration. Burlington got rid of the parterres and knot garden and planted the rear with a rectangular grove of regimented and thickly planted trees. Burlington's trees ended up crowding the house and his new villa. He also planted a thickly wooded strip along the Bollo Brook (down at the bottom of the dip on your left), to give his garden privacy.

Walk 100 metres down the central avenue, still imagining a thick plantation of trees on either side, to the intersection of three avenues, or *patte d'oie*.

The three avenues were laid out one at a time, *ad hoc*. Nevertheless, the result had a strong theatrical flavour. Burlington started in 1716 by asking a leading architect of the day, almost certainly James Gibbs (see p.250), to design a small building, a 'Domed Building', for the end of the original Jacobean avenue, where it reached the end of the old horse pasture. Limes were the fashionable standard trees for avenues. Pleased with the result, the following year Burlington asked the Palladian exponent, Colen Campbell (see p.250), to act as

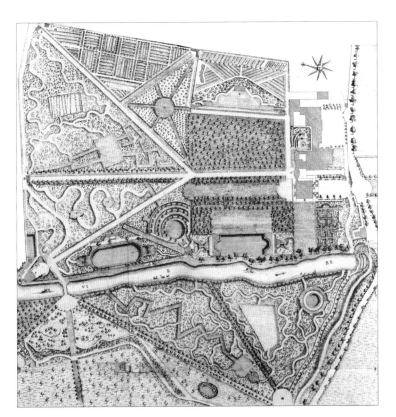

Rocque's plan of 1736 indicates the complexity of a garden that had evolved piecemeal over the previous 20 years.

his tutor in the design of another vista building, a *bagnio* or 'bath', which was duly constructed at the end of an avenue laid half left. In 1719, a couple of years after his second trip to Italy, Burlington designed a Rustic Arch for an avenue running half right. These two outer avenues he lined with high yew hedges, which gave a contrasting darkness to the building at the end of each vista.

Two of these three buildings have now disappeared. The Bagnio and the Domed Building and their respective avenues were both demolished by the Devonshires who sought a more natural and less

LEFT: *the Domed Building, a dumpy depiction, and* RIGHT: *Burlington's bagnio, 'first essay of His Lordship's happy invention', both by Rocque.*

classicist garden. The Venetian window now standing at the end of the resuscitated central avenue was taken from one of the late eighteenth century wings demolished in the 1950s. The Rustic Arch at the end of the right avenue is the sole original surviving feature. The left and right avenues of the '*patte d'oie*' are asymmetric, both in angle and in length. Between the avenues, Burlington planted trees and shrubs to form a Wilderness. Unfortunately, the left (west) avenue was realigned on the stone bridge, in 1959, to the left of where the Bagnio had stood. Partly because the avenue dips at the end, one ends up with no focal point for the vista. It cries out to be rectified and the old focal point re-established.

Walk just to the right of the right hand avenue, through the brief alley to the Doric Column.

The Doric Column was designed by Burlington, possibly even before he built his Rustic Arch. Rather than the present surrounding flowerbeds (the work of Georgiana's husband), six alleys radiated out from a small circus for the Column, each bordered by two metre high yew hedges. Each hedge was terminated at the centre, appropriately, by a term. The column was crowned with a copy of the Venus de Medici (in the Uffizi Gallery, Florence). The column is barren without her.

Turn right to the Deer House.

This, too, Burlington probably built in c.1720, to service the small adjoining paddock, between the ha-ha and the eastern edge of the estate. The ha-ha, as a gardening device in England, is first mentioned in 1712. You may safely speculate, therefore, that this is a strong candidate as the earliest surviving ha-ha. Later, after the deer were moved onto the newly acquired ground west of the Bollo Brook, Kent and Burlington cut the slope in terraces. At the back they built an orangery, which has not survived.

The Orangery, with the Deer House on the left and the ha-ha in the foreground.

Continue along the side of the ha-ha to Inigo Jones's Gateway.

This gateway was about the last addition Burlington made to his gardens. Designed by Jones for Beaufort House, Chelsea in 1621, Burlington was given it in 1738. It was a highly treasured item and served as a gateway to the second orange garden, which had replaced the deer paddock.

Turn around and walk half right across the greensward back to the heel of the _patte d'oie_ and take the left avenue to look down on the Ionic Temple and Orange Tree Garden. Take a seat on the bank if you can.

It seems to have been as a result of his second visit to Italy, in 1719, that Burlington decided his garden should not simply be a series of vistas but a real attempt to imitate the gardens of the Ancients. This temple, based on that of Romulus in Rome, was unlike anything in English gardens of the day.

The feature here, comprising pool, obelisk and temple, was built at the same time as the house, in the mid-1720s, but has little geographical relationship either with the house or, indeed, with the original avenues. The clue to its curious position lies in two factors. First, it was designed when the Bollo Brook behind was still the estate boundary. Second, on either side of it, backing onto the brook was a rectangular pool with either a rounded or apse-like end. These can be seen on Rocque's map of 1736 (see p.143). The two pools were not destined to last and were among the very first features of the garden to be filled in after Burlington's death. The Orange Tree Garden, with its obelisk sitting in a circular pool, must have been an afterthought, squeezed into the available space, as one can see from Rocque's map. Each summer, dozens of orange trees in tubs were set out upon the grassy terraces.

It is time to turn to Burlington's great collaborator here, William Kent. Kent had already met Burlington during the latter's visit to Italy in 1714. He returned to London with Burlington at the end of the latter's second visit in 1719. Kent had spent a whole decade in study in Italy and despite different casts of character the two formed a deep friendship based on their mutual aesthetic interests. He now virtually lived in the Burlington household and was commissioned by Burlington to help emulate the 'gardens of the Ancients', integrating the villa visually with the garden.

Following acquisition of the estate on the far side of the Bollo in 1727, Kent cleared the wooded section along this edge of the stream, to open up a view of the far side, from which side the Ionic Temple suddenly seemed to face the wrong way, uphill rather than out across the lower ground. So a rear doorway was added.

Decades later this was Georgiana's favourite spot in the garden, and she would surround herself by some of the great luminaries of the day, for example Fox, Chatham, Burke, Pitt, Sheridan, Brougham and Canning.

Retrace your steps to the central avenue and walk across the lawn on the right of the house to reach the path crossing the foot of the lake.

Burlington had sandwiched a 'maze', in fact a network of dense trimmed hedges, between the forecourt to his new villa and the Bollo Brook. It was a conservative feature, belonging more to the seventeenth century than the eighteenth. Kent banished it in favour of a lawn rolling down to the stream, ornamented with a few 'naturally planted' trees. It is the first hint that Kent was interested in a pictorial landscape rather than herbaceous gewgaws. As Walpole later remarked, Kent 'leapt the fence and saw that all nature was a garden.'

But it is at the foot of the lake that one can start to appreciate the extent of Kent's vision. Kent was given the newly acquired land beyond the brook, to design as an *avant garde* garden. First, he converted the Bollo into a lake by excavation and damming. Initially it was rectangular but then slightly remodelled to be serpentine. He used the spoil from the lake to raise a terrace on the one hand to shield the new garden from the public gaze on Burlington Lane and on the other, to create the illusion inside that the garden had no boundary wall.

Then, in 1738, he introduced a 'cascade', built into the side of the terrace he had raised. The hydraulics for the Cascade proved a failure, but then the idea of a cascade *in opposition to* the flow of water should have provided its own common sense warning.

A more practical man might have worked with the grain of nature and built a shallower cascade to announce the Bollo Brook's entry to the north end of the serpentine.

Mount the Terrace by the path on the left of the Cascade and walk its length.

This was part of Burlington's favourite garden promenade on which to take his guests, albeit from the other direction. In Burlington's day there was, of course, no school or housing, instead a view across the flood meadow to the river and its traffic, a visual source of enjoyment among the gentry class. As for the terrace itself, in Defoe's words:

> 'for a Defence to his Gardens on that side, and is planted to the Road with all manner of sweet Shrubs, Roses, Honeysuckles etc that yield in season a delightful fragrance…'

Descend to the Obelisk and heel of Kent's *patte d'oie*.

The obelisk incorporates a carved relief, a Roman marriage scene, given Burlington by the Earl of Arundel, who had established the first collection of ancient sculpture in Britain. Between the three avenues stood two terms, adding formality to this entrance. Unfortunately the left-hand avenue was incorrectly aligned when replanted in the mid-1990s.

Walk down the central avenue towards the temple.

On either side of the avenues of his *patte d'oie*, Kent laid winding paths between hedges and small lawns, thought to be characteristic of Pliny's gardens. These have now gone, but could always be revived. Kent deliberately aligned the central avenue on the Ionic

Temple, and one can see immediately how necessary the rear porch is, giving visual sense to the avenue.

Turn left along the side of the lake and proceed to the bridge.

The bridge was built in 1774 for the 5th Duke of Devonshire, probably by James Wyatt, one of the most fashionable architects of his day. It replaced a wooden one.

Take the right avenue (which once led to the Bagnio) back to the heel of Burlington's *patte d'oie*. Turn sharp left to walk up the central avenue half way and turn in to the trees on your right.

A little to your left you will see an open glade, 'the Bowling Green'. Designed probably in the early 1730s, it has the poetic feeling of a rural dell and the architectural feel of a cathedral, its pillars sweet chestnuts.

When you have drunk your fill, retrace your steps to the Exedra, just to the right of the central avenue as you approach the house.

The Exedra, which became the prime focal point of the garden, was one of the last works Kent carried out in the garden, during the years 1736 to 1742. He felled a section of the west part of the grove and created an amphitheatre lawn, edged with cypresses and stone urns, closed at the far end by an 'Exedra', a semicircular hedge. The antique Roman statues, obtained by Burlington in Italy, looked good against the darkness of yew (those you now see are replicas, the originals being indoors). In the words of a contemporary, Robert Morris, 'ancient Romans planted their plots in this rural manner and their temples dedicated to their peculiar Gods, were dispersed among the Groves and woods, which art or nature had made, with vistas to them.' This was what Kent and Burlington had in mind.

Walk across the grass to the path down the left side of the Deer House, leading to the conservatory. Take a seat.

One is immediately struck by the total contrast with the earlier gardens. The 6th Duke of Devonshire acquired and demolished the late seventeenth century Moreton Hall in 1812. If you suspect vandalism, look at the illustration (p.137). When John Evelyn saw building in progress, he thought the house 'somewhat thick and heavy, and not so well understood,' and

> '… the garden much too narrow, the place without water, near a highway, and near another great house of my lord Burlington, little land about it, so that I wonder at the expense; but women will have their will.'

The woman in question was its over-enthusiastic owner.

Devonshire commissioned Samuel Ware, forerunner to the more famous Decimus Burton and Joseph Paxton, to design this conservatory. The original dome, made with cast-iron ribs and columns was unprecedented, over a decade before Fowler's at Syon (see p.70). It was reconstructed as a sixteen-sided pavilion in 1933. You will have seen Ware's work before but possibly not noticed it. Every time you nip into Burlington Arcade for a little routine shopping or admire some painting in the Royal Academy, the backdrop is his handiwork. Back to Chiswick, where it was the *size* of the structure that was sensational: over 92 metres in length, remarkable for its day. It was filled with a remarkable collection of camellias, some ten of these surviving from those supplied in the 1820s. The duke also commissioned John Kennedy to lay out an Italian garden in front.

John Kennedy merits a minor digression: Kennedy inherited his

father's partnership in the renowned horticultural firm, Lee &
Kennedy, established in 1745 and by 1822 'unquestionably the first
nursery in Britain, or, the world.' John Kennedy's own claim to fame
lies less with his work on the Italian garden at Chiswick, than with
the Empress Josephine in France, herself a passionate gardener.
He became her gardening adviser. Extraordinarily he managed
to travel to and fro despite the war between Britain and France,
supplying her with choice items for her garden at Malmaison.
Both governments seemed to acknowledge horticulture as
unquestionably above war and politics. In return Kennedy imbibed
Josephine's passion for roses and introduced the standard rose tree
to Britain. Roses entered their hey-day in the nineteenth century
garden. Here, then, you see the consequence of Kennedy's
horticultural liaison with the Empress Josephine.

**Walk away from the conservatory down the central path
across the garden. On arrival at the sundial, make for the
old gateway to Moreton Hall, half left through the trees.**

You find yourself on the original Burlington Lane, the present main
road another 50 metres away.

**If you wish to visit Hogarth House turn left and left again into
Dukes Avenue (the wide walk running along the east side of
the Chiswick House estate) and follow it to the Great West
Road. Turn right. Hogarth's house is about 250 metres along.**

**If you do not wish to visit Hogarth House, turn right and
follow the old lane.**

If you keep an eye on the base of the much repaired wall on your
right, you will see traces of old red brickwork in English bond,
which is probably a remnant of the original wall to Moreton Hall.

Meanwhile the bank opposite is what one would expect bordering an old lane. The present path leaves the route of the old lane to weave around the modern café.

Follow the path till it brings you back to the main entrance to the gardens.

AFTERWORD

The house and grounds were let as a private lunatic asylum from 1893 until 1928, then acquired by the local authority in 1929. The whole estate was in a state of acute neglect. The pedimented stable block (see the illustration, p.137) was demolished in 1933. In the 1950s the late Georgian wings were demolished, returning Burlington's villa to its original Palladian integrity and escaping the substantial refurbishment costs. Throughout the 1950s major restoration work was carried out on the various structures in the grounds.

Hogarth House
(Open daily except Mondays from 1pm. Closes 5 pm Tuesday to Friday, 6pm weekends and Bank Holiday Mondays.)

This was Hogarth's country retreat and despite the terrible din of traffic beyond its walls, it is still just possible to re-capture in one's mind the essentially rural quality of his retreat. The mulberry tree dates from Hogarth's time.

Hogarth (1697-1764) acquired this house in 1749. Himself childless, he made mulberry tarts for local children, something somehow consistent with his particular contribution to English art.

Hogarth House still in its village setting, Thomas Matthew Rooke, 1897.

Hogarth came from humble origins and was partly self-taught, having started his career as an apprenticed engraver. Hogarth loathed almost all – but especially the foreign tastes – that his neighbour, Lord Burlington, stood for. In 1724 he produced an engraving entitled 'The Taste of Town' which lampooned not only Burlington but also Kent, of whom he remarked, 'never was there a more wretched dauber that soonest got into the palaces of this country.' Hogarth remains England's greatest visual satirist, William Hazlitt reckoning him 'second only to Shakespeare as a student of human comedy.'

Barnes to Hammersmith via Chiswick and back

Distance 8 km: 2.5 hours

This walk commences at Barnes Bridge but if you come by car, take Riverside Drive off Alexandra Avenue to park on the Duke's Meadows promenade. The towpath on this route is never inundated. On the Middlesex bank one walks in the footsteps of great men. Skip their vignettes, if you wish. On the return upstream on the Surrey bank, you are largely spared the author's observations.

Two important sites lie close to the river: Chiswick House and Hogarth's house. Both deserve a separate and more leisurely outing (Walk No 5).

Start by crossing Barnes railway bridge to the Middlesex bank and turn right along the Promenade/towpath. Walk to the bandstand and shelters.

Traditionally the flood meadows along this stretch were probably entirely given over to osier beds (see p.223), with agricultural land, orchards and market gardens, further back from the river. The shallow terracing, the bandstand and two shelters of Duke's Meadows were built following a council decision in 1923 to purchase the meadows and make them available for community use. This ended more than two decades of proposals for 'developing' these lands, which previously belonged to the Duke of Devonshire. The first proposal, in 1902, was for a massive housing development, named Burlingwick – an unfortunate conflation of the names

Burlington and Chiswick. Had it happened this whole area from Barnes Bridge to Chiswick House would have been covered in housing for a nice class of person, as the *Chiswick Times* reassured its readers:

> 'Burlingwick is not proposed to house.... the POOR, OR WORKING CLASSES.... No, Burlingwick will maintain the present character of Chiswick .... for the well-to-do and better class.'

Mr Jonathan Carr, who had masterminded that paragon of suburban elegance, Bedford Park, was appointed to plan the project. Mercifully, the proposal ran into problems, principally because access to the metropolis was too poor for that nicer class of person the developers wished to attract. By 1911 the project had fallen into abeyance. Two years later there was another scare when the Brentford Gas Company proposed erecting a major gas works on the meadows. War intervened, but the company renewed its interest in 1919. Local residents were appalled and it seems that as part of their riposte, in an attempt perhaps to strike a positive note, another housing estate was proposed for 360 workers' dwellings, with blocks of flats facing Mortlake, but also with a riverside tree-lined promenade and, further back from the river, orchards and playing fields.

Neither proposal prevailed. Instead, the local authority purchased the meadows from the duke and struck a deal with the Riverside and Ballast Company (essentially the same people as at Ham, see vol. I, p. 136) to extract the river gravel in five acre sections, each section to be re-filled as they worked their way along. The Company paid £1,500 per acre (over £40,000 per acre in today's terms). It was a lot less generous with its workforce which, it seems, started at 6am, broke for two hours, 5-7pm for a meal, and continued till midnight. Many of the men slept on site, completing an 85-hour week at a rate, in today's terms, of less than £1.50 per hour. By 1937, when the workings closed, two million cubic yards of gravel and sand had been extracted and used, for example, for the new Bank of England buildings. In the meantime, in keeping with a land fit for heroes, the newly formed British Legion played patriotic and light classical numbers in the bandstand.

At the end of the open greensward take to the tarmac path if you are not already on it. On your left, look out for a bijou white building with a pitched roof.

This is the Bollo Brook Sluice House. The Bollo Brook rises on Hanger Hill, Ealing and arrives via Acton. In the nineteenth century the stream was piped through the lake in Chiswick House Gardens, which it had previously filled, and since the 1930s runs in a pipe under the sluice house to debouche into the Thames. A second pipe runs *from* the Thames beneath the sluice house to Chiswick House lake. At high water the sluice can be opened to replenish the level of the lake. A drive leads away from the river, past a row of houses. These houses, an early twentieth century 'model' estate, stand on sewage works that were built here in the second half of the nineteenth century.

Shortly after, on your right, you will pass a line of almost two dozen Lombardy poplars.

Lombardy poplars are highly distinctive on account of their tall columnar habit. They were introduced to Britain in the mid-eighteenth century. They are always planted and have never naturalised themselves. Once mature, they have a habit of shedding branches in high winds, leaving a tall stump from which new shoots renew the cycle. Oliver Rackham, the eminent countryside historian, observes that the Lombardy poplar is 'always male and incapable of looking after itself'. No comment.

Corney House with its gazebo overlooking the river. In the background stands St Nicholas' Church. Jacob Knyff, c. 1675.

The riverside path runs in front of a new development, Corney Reach.

These are the grounds of Corney House, home to the Russells (family name of the future Earls of Bedford) from 1542 to 1663. Corney is a corruption of 'cornhythe', indicative not only of the crops grown behind the meadows, but also that somewhere here stood a medieval wharf. The house was demolished by the Devonshires in 1832.

Make your way past the front of Corney Reach, past Chiswick Pier on your right.

Chiswick Pier Trust provides valuable moorings and other facilities for river users. Such ventures keep alive human engagement with the Thames and deserve to be cherished.

Proceed along the riverbank towards the heart of old Chiswick.

The name Chiswick probably derives from 'cheese dairy farm' or village. In 1845 it was reported that:

'within the last hundred years a very considerable mart,

John Thornycroft with his steam launch Nautilus No. 1 Boat, *at Church Wharf, in front of Slut's Hole, Chiswick, 1860.*

or fair, for cheese, was annually held in the field called the Great Downs nearly opposite the Duke of Devonshire's.'
If this memory was truly rooted in fact, it probably referred to the downstream end of Duke's Meadows, close to Corney House.

Continue until you come out at the draw-dock at the foot of Church Street. On your left the bland modern houses replaced Church Wharf, where the boatbuilder John Thornycroft made his career. Thornycroft's *Nautilus* (1860), launched here, was the first steam launch able to keep up with racing eights. Adjoining the wharf and clustered at the foot of the graveyard stood the once excitingly named Slut's Hole, rudimentary dwellings where the fisher families lived. The name was sanitised to Fisherman's Place in a fit of middle-class politeness in the mid-nineteenth century. Oh, why can't we just let things be?

Fisherman's Place, or Slut's Hole.

Make a short detour up Church Street.
(If you are determined to visit Chiswick House during the course of this walk, turn left along Powell Walk, just past the church, and cross Burlington Lane, to Chiswick House entrance, see p.135. Retrace your steps afterwards).

Church Street remains the old heart of Chiswick village, now condemned to a backwater as a result of the Great West Road. It boasts Chiswick's most interesting houses and you should explore it until the traffic of Hogarth Roundabout becomes sufficiently unbearable to force you back.

Look to your right on your way away from the river for:
Vine House is late eighteenth century. **Nos. 1 and 2**, now *The Old Burlington*, is a sixteenth century house with an overhanging upper floor, typical of its day.

Lamb Cottage hides its former identity as a pub behind weather-boarding. Behind it stands the old **Lamb brewery** building. Its tower on top contained a water tank, the water lifted by steam engine from a borehole, only one of two surviving breweries with this design. **Brampton House**, **Ferry House**, **Wisteria House** and **Post Office House** are all eighteenth century.

(If you feel particularly brave or deaf, **Chiswick Square**, tucked just around to your left on Burlington Lane, offers a handsome composition of late seventeenth century mansions, the central one, **Boston House** re-fronted in the 1740s.)

Otherwise, turn around when the noise of the main road drives you back. Continue looking to your right as you return to the river.

Pages Yard is a restored group of seventeenth century cottages. **Latimer House** and **Holly House** were once a single eighteenth century dwelling.

The parish church of St Nicholas

Alas, St Nicholas, like so many churches, was almost entirely rebuilt in the late nineteenth century. Its mid-fifteenth century hammer-beam roof of oak and chestnut was replaced with pine, due to a mistaken fit of penny-pinching. Its eighteenth century box pews also went. Only the fifteenth century tower survives. At least the re-building of the church was carried out by an expert, J.L. Pearson, whose next job was the restoration of Westminster Hall. So if you want an internal glimpse of good neo-Perpendicular, catch the church when it is usually open, on Sunday afternoons. Many notable figures were buried in the churchyard, for example: Barbara Villiers, mistress to Charles II, Lord Burlington, William Kent, William Hogarth. When Barbara Villiers died in 1709, she was attended at St Nicholas by two dukes and four peers of the realm as her pallbearers. You would have to be a pretty sensational mistress to get that kind of treatment today.

Inside the church on the right (south) wall of the Lady Chapel is the memorial to Thomas Chaloner and his wife. Chaloner discovered (and in 1600 opened) the first alum mines in Britain at his estate in Yorkshire. Alum was extremely valuable for making dyes fast, sufficiently so that Charles I later decided to seize the mines for the Crown. By then Chaloner was dead but his son, also Thomas, was predictably incensed. It very probably influenced his decision as a judge to sign Charles' death warrant in 1649. So think about the longer term before snatching other folk's toys. On your way out, note to the left of the door a delightful 1930s ceramic Cristes Cheste alms box bedded into the wall.

The Graveyards

Inside the church precinct, if you admire William Hogarth (see p.152 for his house), you will wish to doff your cap to his tomb, crowned with a funerary urn, just below the church. Hogarth, if anyone, would have enormously enjoyed the view he was given, right over Slut's Hole and its daily round: the very essence of ordinary earthy humanity. Next door is the railed-in altar tomb of Richard Wright, Burlington's bricklayer at Chiswick House. If you wish to stray further, the much larger graveyard contains a variety of interesting graves. Of these perhaps the most notable is that of the painter, James McNeill Whistler (1834-1903) an American who was hugely influential on British art during his lifetime.

Chiswick Mall is a treat. Here are some brief notes as appropriate:
Bedford House, named after a house built by the Russells after they
    left Corney House, was home to the actor Michael Redgrave and
    his family, 1945-54.

Unloading barges off Chiswick drawdock. Note the carts backed down into the river for the transference of goods.

Red Lion House was formerly an inn.

The site of the **Griffin Brewery**, on the corner of the Mall and Chiswick Lane South has been associated with brewing since the late seventeenth century. By the mid-eighteenth century the brewery obtained the lease on several local pubs, for example the *Bull's Head* at Strand-on-the Green, and thus ensured a ready market for its beer. There is nothing particularly special about the name 'Griffin', purloined off a city brewery which had collapsed in 1816. Fuller is the family name associated with the brewery since the 1820s, and 'London Pride' is its rightly celebrated brew. (For more on brewing see p.260.)

On your right lies an old drawdock and, beyond it, Chiswick Eyot itself.
Like virtually every other island on the tidal Thames, Chiswick Eyot has been greatly reduced by the nineteenth century channelling and narrowing of the river from the sluggish stream it once was. In London's anxiety to make everything hurry, we have destroyed much of the sweetness of the Thames. In the mid-nineteenth century the ait

A tea break while osier cutting on Chiswick Eyot.

still covered an area of four acres, but is barely one acre now. It was a farmed osier bed as recently as the 1920s and is now a wildlife reserve. In 1970 the borough proposed demolishing the island completely for the sake of river traffic, but was thwarted by local indignation, the wretched bustlers for once defeated.

On your left after Chiswick Lane South:
Heron House marks the beginning of an extremely handsome
    Victorian terrace of fashionable mansions.
College House, set back, refers to the house that stood here in the
    sixteenth century belonging to Westminster School. It provided
    accommodation for 40 students and their staff in case they had to
    flee plague in Westminster, which by the end of the sixteenth
    century was pretty much part of the growing city. It later became
    the print shop and home for Charles Whittingham (see below).

Greenash, built by John Belcher in 1882 for Sir John Thornycroft, the great innovative boat-builder, whose wharf and internationally famous boat-building business lay just upstream of the church (see p.158).

Orford House and **The Tides**, both dated 1886, stand out as handsome forerunners of the best of Edwardian housing, solid, distinguished, generously proportioned and self-assured in their idea of England. For they *are* deeply English in their loveliness and if you see a house like these, say, in Scotland, you know they have stolen across the border at dead of night. Like Greenash, they were designed by John Belcher, one tile-hung and the other timber-framed gable.

Orford House was built on the site of High House, where a printer, Charles Whittingham, came to work in 1809. He became obsessive about print and paper quality and was the first to introduce 'India paper' for books. He had started his business in Fetter Lane in 1789. He came here partly in order to purchase old tar ropes from passing junk barges. These would have been unloaded at one of the two draw-docks. He extracted the tar for ink and broke up the hemp to manufacture fine silky paper. His ink became renowned for its brilliance and excellence. His 'Chiswick Press' became internationally famous for its high quality pocket-sized publications, to the distress of publishing competitors. He used a steam engine to make the paper pulp and ran steam pipes off it to warm the workshops. But he never used the engine for printing. Much better done by hand press, he maintained, and his reputation spread far and wide. The Chiswick Press lasted for over a century. It heralds a stretch of riverbank notable for some of the finest literary and publishing activities of the nineteenth century.

Walpole House. Early eighteenth century brickwork and bracketed eaves to the main projecting parts hide a house of Tudor origin, apparently where Barbara Villiers lived. The porch with fluted Corinthian pilasters is eighteenth century. In 1796 Daniel O'Connell, one of the great early Irish nationalists, lived here as a law student. He played a crucial role in the Catholic emancipation of 1829, having been elected MP for Co. Clare the previous year but debarred from Parliament on account of his faith. During the 1820s, Walpole House was a horrid little prep school. Thackeray, an unhappy inmate, had his revenge by caricaturing it as Miss Pinkerton's Seminary for Young Ladies in *Vanity Fair*. If you like wrought iron, here is an example to be admired.

Morton House, c.1700, was also re-fronted c.1735, and skilfully rebuilt in the 1950s when, alarmingly, it began to bulge. It was home to Eric Kennington, the artist who made his name with his illustrations to T.E Lawrence's *The Seven Pillars of Wisdom*.

On the right, at the end of Chiswick Mall, stands St Peter's Wharf, staggered small dwellings true to their period, c.1975, and neatly done.

Continue to Hammersmith Terrace. This utterly urban terrace, dating from 1750, is remarkable. When constructed it stood alone in open countryside. The frontages face the river. A quarter of a century before its construction Daniel Defoe had already foreseen Hammersmith's inevitable urbanisation:

> '... in this village we see now not only a wood of great houses and palaces, but a noble square built as it were in the middle of several handsome streets, as if the village seemed inclined to grow up into a city. Here we are told they design to obtain the grant of a market, though it be so near to London, and some talk also of building a fine stone bridge over the Thames...'

Between 1800 and 1830 the number of both inhabitants and dwellings in Hammersmith doubled.

Look out for the blue plaques that will soon render the houses without them an endangered species. This is where book production takes over.

A.P. Herbert (1890-1971), author and wit. In 1935 he became MP for Oxford University, a seat he held until its suppression in 1950. He was an independent, acting on conscience and common sense, free from the deadening grip of party control. In his autobiography, APH tells how he came to live here:

'…. on Boat Race Day I would journey out to Duke's Meadows, below Barnes Bridge on the Middlesex side, and bellow: "Oxford! Ox*ford*." One year – it must have been 1913 – I was introduced on the bank to a little old man… the famous F.Anstey [Anstey Guthrie, author of humorous works, e.g. *Vice Versa* (1882)]… After the race I was going to take a bus back to Kensington, but the great man said: "No. Come with me. I will show you a nice walk." I went with him eagerly and he walked me along the water fronts of Chiswick and Hammersmith, the best part of two miles….'

Three years later, in January 1916, APH was married and back in London, having been wounded in the ill-starred Dardenelles campaign:

'…. my wife and I were looking for a home…. Suddenly I thought of the little old man. We took a bus to Hammersmith and walked westward from the Bridge. We looked longingly at Kelmscott House, with its spacious garden… We walked on, excited by the scene; and lo, over the door of No. 12 Hammersmith Terrace was an estate agent's TO LET board. I do not think such a thing has been seen in the Terrace from that day to this. With the help of some kind folk at No 11 we burgled the house at once, and took it the next day, at a rent of £55 per annum. In February we moved in, and I went back to the Division in France. See, then, how much I owe to the rowing men who lured me to the Duke's Meadow, and to Accident that led me to Anstey.'

Emery Walker (1851-1933) had to leave school at 13. After seven years of unskilled labours, he was invited to join the Typographical Etching Company, whose owner had taken a shine to him. After 10 years, in 1886, Walker established his own engraving enterprise close to his home here. It was Walker, giving a lantern slide lecture in 1888, who inspired William Morris to turn his attention to the printed word. Both inveighed against the very low standards of typography of the day. Walker's passion was for the unadorned elegance of ordinary books. If books do furnish your room, tread with a grateful step for as his biographer wrote half a century ago:

'It is scarcely too much to say that his influence, direct or indirect, can be discerned in nearly every well-designed page of type that now appears, and that to him more than to any other man this century's great improvement in book production has been due.'

In the words of the Printer to the University of Oxford, 'Walker was perhaps the last of the great Victorians'.

Edward Johnston (1872-1944) acquired a fascination with illuminating as a teenager and became a seminal teacher of calligraphy and lettering. We gaze at Johnston's work on an almost daily basis, for he redesigned the London Underground's roundel and lettering, pretty much the symbol for London itself.

Follow the path back to the riverbank. The Walkway, with its small green and playground, was created in 1960, on the site of the old

West Middlesex Water Works.

West Middlesex Water Works (the arcaded wall at the back is its last vestige) and downstream of it, the extremely noisome oil mills, commemorated in the adjoining street name: Oil Mill Lane.

Keep walking, through the short passage. On your left, look out for:

Linden House, c. 1733 is now home to the London Corinthian Sailing Club, founded as the Corinthian Sailing Club in 1894, at a time when a 'Corinthian' was a gentleman and, therefore, amateur sportsman, who rode his own horses on the turf, or sailed his own yacht. The term goes back at least to the sixteenth century, for Prince Hal exclaims: 'I am no proud Jack, like Falstaff; but a Corinthian, a lad of mettle, a good boy.' (*Henry IV*, Part 1)

On your right, look out for a couple of concave parts of the river wall and embankment. These 'bastions', supposedly, are the last remains of River Court, the house and garden of the Dowager Queen Catherine of Braganza, before she returned to her native Portugal in 1692.

Again, on your left:

No. 26 Kelmscott House. The plaque over the coach house on the left
omits to state that Ronalds, in order to invent a workable electric
telegraph, laid over eight miles of cable in his back garden, dug
out over 50 years later. When he ran hotfoot to the Admiralty
to share his invention in 1816, the First Lord of the Admiralty
poured scorn on the enterprise. After all, what possible use
could there be for such newfangled technology, now that Boney
was defeated? Ronalds was dismissed with the following put-
down: 'telegraphs are now totally unnecessary and no other
[system] than the one in use [semaphore] will be adopted.' So it
is a relief to learn that Ronalds, 'the least pushful of original
inventors,' had a subsequent distinguished career as a meteor-
ologist, becoming director of the Kew Observatory (see p.47).

   The house, however, is much more famous as the residence
of William Morris (1834-1896) and the basement is now a
museum (open 2-5pm, Thursday and Saturday afternoons).
In the words of his biographer, Fiona MacCarthy, he was

   'one of the most prolific Victorian poets. He was the greatest
   artist-craftsman of his period. He ran a successful decor-
   ating and manufacturing business and kept a high profile
   London retail shop. Morris was also a passionate social
   reformer, an early environmentalist, an educationalist, and
   would-be feminist; at the age of fifty he crossed the 'river of
   fire' to become a revolutionary socialist.'

   In fact he believed revolution was the only way of destroying
capitalism and bringing about a socialist society. He used the
coach house first as a tapestry works, then, after his expulsion
from the Socialist League, for the meetings of his own
movement, the Hammersmith Socialist Society. Among those
who came here for the meetings were George Bernard Shaw,
Annie Besant, Keir Hardie, Sidney and Beatrice Webb. The

tragedy for Morris was that his work did not trigger an aesthetic revolution or confer dignity on ordinary working people. Rather, his work adorned the homes of the rich and powerful. But his vision of England remained passionate to the end, one that had no time for Empire, State and Nation:

> 'I am no patriot as the word is generally used; and yet I am not ashamed to say that as for the face of the land we live in I love it with something of the passion of a lover.'

Morris and his wife Janey, model and lover for Daniel Gabriel Rossetti, came here in 1879. He called it Kelmscott House after their beloved manor house in Oxfordshire.

Morris became gripped by his ambition to publish:

> 'I began printing books with the hope of producing some which would have a definite aim of beauty, while at the same time they should be easy to read….I have always been a great admirer of the calligraphy of the Middle Ages, and of the earlier printing which took its place…. And it was the essence of my undertaking to produce books which it would be a pleasure to look upon as pieces of printing and arrangement of type.'

No 21 Upper Mall is where Morris, in the opinion of one admirer, printed 'the finest book ever produced', the Kelmscott *Chaucer*, only a couple of months before his death in 1896. When he was dying, one doctor diagnosed his fatal condition as 'simply being William Morris, and having done more work than most ten men'.

Enter Dove Passage.

'The Dove' pub dates back to 1790, if not earlier.

Nos. 13-15 Dove Passage is the site of Thomas Cobden-Sanderson's (1840-1922) internationally famous bindery, 1893-1921.

Cobden-Sanderson is yet another bookish name to conjure with. Like most successful men, Cobden-Sanderson owed his success to a good woman or, in his case, to two. It was his brand new wife, Anne, who urged him to abandon his legal practice in favour of working with his hands. Good Woman Number Two was his neighbour, Janey Morris, who suggested he learn bookbinding. Ten years later, in 1893, Cobden-Sanderson opened Doves Bindery and 'rapidly established himself as a binder of admirable taste, fecund and versatile in decorative ideas, impeccable in technique, and scrupulous in finish.' Cobden-Sanderson coined the term 'arts and crafts' for the movement in which, with Morris, he played such an important part. And if you ever wondered what the Arts and Crafts Movement really was, its aim, he claimed, was 'to bring all the activities of the human spirit under the influence of one idea, the idea that life is creation, and should be creative in modes of art....'

No. 17, The Seasons, is where Emery Walker and Cobden-Sanderson established the Doves Press and Bindery in 1900. For a while they were close colleagues, producing a fine typeface based on a fifteenth century Venetian font. The drawings were made in Walker's office, then cut at Doves Press. In 1909 there was some very profound falling-out between them and Walker departed. Doves Press finally ceased to be viable in 1916. But to learn of its hilarious end, one must stand on Hammersmith Bridge (see below).

Immediately opposite stands **No. 12, Sussex House**, c.1726, now carefully hidden from view. The left part of it is where Morris first started printing for the Kelmscott Press in 1891. Emery Walker had no capital whereby he could become Morris's partner but gave unstintingly of his knowledge and skill to ensure its success. After Morris had done with the building, Walker

Hammersmith Creek.

used it for his engraving. Where Doves Press was restrained and
austere, the Kelmscott press was florid and baroque.

As you come into Furnival Gardens, it is time to pause. Note the
concrete vent on the river wall. Beneath, a culvert is visible at low
water, an undignified fate for Stamford Brook, which should surely
enter the Thames with greater *éclat*. Once it flowed into Hammersmith Creek. In its heyday, barges used the creek, which reached
as far as King Street. But Stamford Brook was also defiled and by
1899 one would 'run the gauntlet of the disgraceful open sewer,
which was once a purling crystal brooklet'. Having defiled it, we
finally concealed it beneath concrete to hide our shame. A hump-
backed bridge once ran across the creek which, together with the
surrounding wharves, formed the most picturesque attribute of
Hammersmith, once known as 'Little Wapping'. All now gone, the
creek filled with rubble in 1936. Look back across the greensward
and the Great West Road to the Hammersmith town hall, built in
1938-39. It sits exactly where once was the creek. Furnival Gardens

is undeniably pleasant, set against the roar of the road, but there's precious little poetry in the greensward left behind.

You will already have started to wonder who Furnivall can have been, to be immortalised here. F.J. Furnivall (1825-1910) was far larger than life. He was the ultimate enthusiast, passionate about social justice and personal health. He never smoked or drank and, unusually for the age, became a vegetarian. He loathed the growing class system and its exclusions. In 1849 he opened a school for poor men and boys. In 1851 he sold his book collection so as to give £100 to support striking woodcutters. The following year he helped establish the Working Men's Association. But it was his literary work that attracted national attention. In 1861 he started work on a dictionary, which finally saw the light of day as *The Oxford English Dictionary*. Fortunately the task was taken out of his hands, for he had been diverted by new pursuits, founding in 1864 the Early English Texts Society, in 1868 the Chaucer Society, in 1873 the Ballad Society and also the New Shakespeare Society, in 1881 the Wiclif Society and in 1886 the Browning Society and the Shelley Society. Phew. In his spare time he became the leading expert of his day on Chaucer. Kenneth Grahame modelled Ratty on him in *The Wind in the Willows*, and this finally brings us to why Furnivall is immortalised here on the riverbank. To say that Furnivall enjoyed messing about in boats is an understatement.

Continue walking, looking out for the Furnivall Sculling Club to your left, just beyond the Gardens.

Having learnt to scull in his teens, rowing became Furnivall's lifetime obsession. At the age of 20, together with a local waterman, he designed a new sculling boat, narrow in beam and equipped with the newfangled outriggers (see p.240). He sculled regularly. He brought his democratic principles to the river. When, in 1891, the

Frederick Furnivall with his young ladies.

Amateur Rowing Association refused to accept working men as 'amateurs', Furnivall promptly founded the National Amateur Rowing Association (NARA), which anyone could join. At the age of 71 – and this is the bit you have so long been waiting for, for you are standing outside it – Furnivall founded 'the Hammersmith Sculling Club for girls and men'. Forget the men. Furnivall was particularly fond of recruiting pretty young waitresses into the club and showing them how to handle a pair of sculls, something he did very ably every Sunday, when he himself rowed to Richmond and back, a habit he maintained almost to the day he died.

No. 6 is the headquarters of the Amateur Rowing Association. It is worth recalling the crippling snobbery which once surrounded rowing. Together with the Henley Stewards, the ARA effectively blocked Furnivall's NARA from participating at Henley or indeed in any context of 'gentleman' amateurs. In 1920 Grace

Kelly's father, a distinguished sculler, won the Olympic gold, only to be excluded from Henley: 'Sorry, wrong class, old boy.' It was not until 1956 that the two rival associations, ARA and NARA, finally amalgamated.

As you approach the bridge and the traffic noise of the twenty first century, comfort yourself with the memory of Hammersmith's market gardens and nurseries. In the early eighteenth century Hammersmith already had a reputation in the city for strawberries, raspberries, currants and gooseberries. From the late eighteenth century there were still plenty of fields put down to a yearly rotation of, say, potatoes, followed by wheat, followed by clover with a heavy manure. But they progressively gave way to market garden produce. In mid-summer these supplied London with its strawberries. Scores of women would walk from Wales and Shropshire in early June to help carry the fruit to market. The fittest walked from Hammersmith to Covent Garden four times within the day, carrying on their heads 40-50lb baskets of strawberries, then market vegetables. They returned home in September. At the end of the season they might have £10 net profit [about £400 in our terms], and another £5 if they were prepared to work another six weeks on vegetables. But a handful would collapse and die under the strain. They were still walking in the 1830s, when Irish migrant labour started to displace them in the market gardens, a process that continued for the next twenty years.

Hammersmith Bridge

There had been talk of the need for a bridge here as early as 1671, but it had come to nothing. The suspension bridge, the first of its kind for the Thames, was originally built in 1825-27 by William Tierney Clark, engineer to the waterworks a couple of hundred yards upstream. A suspension bridge was an economy measure and this was the second of its kind, the first being across the Tweed near Berwick, 1820. It was only 6 metres wide. The present wider version

The original Hammersmith Bridge.

was built by Joseph Bazalgette on Clark's cutwater piers in 1887.

Walk across on the upstream footpath. Halfway across the bridge you may notice a particularly heavily reinforced 'link' in the bridge suspension. In March 1939 the IRA left a bomb on the bridge. A passer-by, a hairdresser by trade, spotted it and with great valour hurled it into the river. It went off, hurting no one, but damaging this link of the bridge, which consequently needed strengthening.

Find a seat on the bridge while you read.

A sheep was roasted on the ice near here in the awesome winter of 1838 for the benefit of 'distressed watermen'. The immediate cause for distress was the frozen river, which left water families with no income at all. But the sheep had been donated by the firm which had built the masonry for the bridge and that hinted at the underlying cause for long-term decline. The bridge meant that the market gardeners who created the principal wealth of Barnes and Mortlake no longer depended on water transport. A large tent was erected on the ice in the middle of the river on the downstream side of the bridge. Thousands lined the banks, or watched from the bridge. The generous paid to enter the tent and taste the meat. The proceeds were distributed among the distressed.

But before you succumb to a fit of melancholy, enjoy the following account of disarming and delightful incompetence. On 28th October 1916 Cobden-Sanderson, *doyen* of the Doves Press, wrote in his journal:

> 'This evening I have done an extraordinary thing, which may have consequences.... Well, what I have done is this: I went out at sundown to "bequeath" a page of type [the *forme* – the lead face in its wooden chase, or frame] to the "bed of the river" – but it alighted, not on the bed of the river but on a ledge of the far pier of the bridge, and is there now. The tide is ebbing, and there it will remain all the night.... My idea was magnificent; the act ridiculous.'

5th November he recorded another fiasco:

> 'On Friday night I threw two packets of type ... from the bridge, aiming at the river, but they alighted one after the other on a projecting level ledge of the southernmost pier of the bridge, and there remain, visible, inaccessible, irremovable by me.... It was all too ridiculous... Anyhow, I have not yet been collared by the Thames Commissioners... And I am now on my guard, and throw only type, and clear of the bridge.... I had tried various ways of carrying the type, which is always heavy... Arrived at the bridge I cross to the other side, take a stealthy look round, and if no one is in sight, I heave the box to the parapet, release the sliding lid, and let the type fall sheer into the river... The wind is still raging, the earth still revolves, and still tirelessly is sweeping on its course round the sun; and in this great theatre of events I sit up and write my adventure, "bequeathing" the Doves type to the Thames.'

Someone else, a certain Kate Webster, had far greater success in consigning an unwanted item to the deep, but her story can wait.

Pause as you reach the far end of the bridge.

You will be mesmerised by the armorial field-day Bazalgette had at each end of the bridge. Apart from the Royal Arms, you may familiarise yourself clockwise with the arms of the counties of Kent (the rampant white horse); Guildford, on behalf of all Surrey; the City of Westminster; Colchester, on behalf of all Essex; Middlesex; and the City of London. Given Colchester, you may well be wondering why not Truro, Rutland or Penrith?

Turn sharp right, down onto the towpath.

Before walking upstream you may care to know a little about the land on this side of the river. If not, move on to the next paragraph. Obtaining sufficient land opposite Hammersmith for the projected bridge had not been easy, but eventually a deal was struck to purchase the Barn Elms Estate, which covered most of the Barnes peninsula.

Initially the plan was to drive the road straight to, and through, Barnes pond. A shareholder whose house faced onto Barnes Green suddenly saw how undesirable that might be and persuaded against it, and the Castelnau route was adopted. (Castelnau is named after the ancestral Huguenot estate of the developer.) The land was very marshy, having long consisted of osier beds, known locally as 'twyghawes' or 'twygaits'.

The approach to the bridge had to be built up, so they used spoil from St Katherine's Dock, by the Tower of London, for the ramp here. Until the end of the nineteenth century glass-fronted stalls displayed freshly picked local strawberries to tempt passers-by.

Immediately opposite the ramp lie the buildings and playing fields of St Paul's School. The playing fields cover two major reservoirs dug in 1838 for the West Middlesex Waterworks, but filled in a century later. The school settled here in 1968, roughly a millennium after the manor of Barnes was granted to the Dean and Chapter of St Paul's Cathedral by the Saxon monarch, Athelstan, c.930. The school itself was founded in 1509 by John Colet, Dean of St Paul's, providing free education for *parvuli Christe* as he touchingly called the pupils, to be 'of all nations and countries indifferently'. The first school building perished in the Great Fire of 1666. The school moved to Hammersmith in 1884 before crossing to the Surrey bank.

Start walking upstream but look out for a giant of a tree on your left about 150m upstream from the Bridge.

Because of their mass, black poplars often stood as boundary markers and you will notice, if you keep your eye out for them, that they follow the boundary on your left, the boundary of the manor of Barnes.

In earlier times these would have been native black poplars (these rarities may be seen on Walk No. 7). This specimen, and others along this stretch are all (save one) hybrid Italian black poplars, planted in the nineteenth century. Described by at least one distinguished naturalist as 'characterless', I disagree. The larger ones, like the one standing before you, are massive, majestic and magnificent. They rightly inspire awe. They also stand as a rebuke to the arid and truly characterless towpath.

There are still some varieties of wildflower that manage to grow along here, but by taming the riverbank we have lost many species and, almost as bad, we have lost the rich, reckless and promiscuous profusion there once was: large flowered bitter cress, small marsh valerian, persicary, mouse-eared chickweed, tawny flowered touch-me-not, broad-leafed water parsnip and many more besides. All we have left is the poetry of their names. They are the items here on the charge sheet against our destructiveness. We could and should surely do better to render the riverbank not only more interesting but also a more welcoming habitat for wildlife. And if we must wear gumboots, it is a very small price to pay.

Look out for Lonsdale Reservoir on your left. Its boundary is lined with intermittent hybrid black poplars. This was dug as a settling reservoir to improve domestic water quality in 1838, enlarged in 1879 and only decommissioned in 1960. It was dug out of 'West Mead', the flood meadow that was once here. It is now a nature reserve, well worth a brief detour at one of the gaps in the iron fence, and a place where wild flowers may still flourish. Look out for fallen black poplar branches. One or two of these are truly massive, and offer the opportunity for regeneration.

Continue walking. A narrowing strip of park lies between the Thames towpath and Lonsdale Road as they converge. Look out for the drawdock, a ramp down to the water on your right, the Small Profit Dock.

Lonsdale Road started off from Castelnau in an arc towards Barnes Terrace in 1828, but it was still a road to nowhere, for it was bitterly opposed by a Miss Hibbert who lived in a large mansion a few metres upstream and who had no wish for a road running in front of her house. Barnes Vestry was also opposed, for the road would interfere with the village drawdock, which led straight into the High Street and the heart of the village. Both Miss Hibbert and the Vestry were neatly bypassed. The Hammersmith Bridge committee simply got the City of London to agree to running the end of the projected road into the towpath, which it already owned, and arbitrarily to remove the Barnes drawdock, since it owned the river. It proposed to replace the old drawdock with a new one at 'Small Profit', a narrow strip of common land. The Vestry knew when it

Barnes Bridge, built in 1849, showing the single track line before it was reinforced. Although the drawdock must have been removed by the time of this illustration, there is a strong suggestion that barges still used the foreshore here at low water.

had been outmanoeuvred and gave way. Miss Hibbert did not. She was still objecting in 1833, magnificently but to no avail. After her death, her estate was purchased by the Earl of Lonsdale as a weekend resort. The road was named after him in 1858. That's class and gender deference for you. I'm calling it Hibbert Road from now on.

Keep walking (if you are still feeling full of energy, Barnes Green up the High Street to your left merits a detour). The old police station stands on the site of a late eighteenth century brewery, now nicely bracketed by a couple of elegant modern additions. Almost next door stands the *Bull's Head*, famous for its jazz. There has been a public house here since 1649 if not earlier, patronized by watermen and halers.

Walk along the Terrace.

The Terrace became extremely fashionable, particularly for summer holiday lets, in the early nineteenth century. It seems an incongruous setting, therefore, for a dark and unsavoury tale. Steel yourself. It is along the shingle here at low water that a box was washed up in March 1879. It contained a mass of flesh, which proved to be part of a woman's body. The skin was the texture of parchment and there was no decomposition leading to the conclusion that the flesh had been boiled. The head and one leg were missing. The body was identified as that of a missing Richmond resident. It was her maid, Kate Webster, who had committed the foul deed. She had thrown her mistress down the stairs, chopped her up and boiled the principal part, scooping off the fat, which she sold to neighbours as dripping. That is the part that upsets. She had launched the box from Richmond Bridge. She put the leg in a black bag, which she threw over Hammersmith Bridge. It was never recovered. A foot was found in a Twickenham dung heap. The head was never found. (It has got to be knocking around somewhere.) Webster was hanged that July.

On your left, No. 10 was home for four years to Gustav Holst (1874-1934). Holst had moved from Richmond to Barnes in 1909. In his maturity Holst produced 'compositions of incomparable sureness of touch and clarity of texture' but you might wonder how he achieved this in the light of the wonderful opening line to a letter he wrote at his desk here on the Terrace:

> 'I would rather have a sympathetic conductor with no orchestra than *vice versa*.'

It makes you think.

Hammersmith to Putney and back

Distance 8 km: 2.5 hours

This walk explores the Middlesex and Surrey riverbanks between Hammersmith and Putney bridges. Its climax, just before turning back along the Surrey bank, is Fulham Palace. You may wish to make a special outing for Fulham Palace, after refurbishment of part of the building in 2005-6, and for All Saints' Church, next door.

Descend from Hammersmith Bridge on the Middlesex bank and turn downstream along the riverbank.

This stretch of riverbank in the direction of Fulham was heavily industrialised during the nineteenth century. In the middle of the century Queen's Wharf was established, a name still borne by the building beyond the drawdock. Next door stood an electricity works, 1897, one of the earliest providers of power to the public, only closed in 1965.

Turn left when compelled and at the earliest opportunity turn right, into Crisp Road.

Crisp Road commemorates the principal local magnate of his day. Nicholas Crisp made his pile trading slaves out of Guinea, where Charles I had granted him a monopoly. He also developed the local brick industry. Parliament tried to tax Crisp, so he naturally joined the Royalist cause. All his property confiscated by the Commonwealth, he lived quietly in Hammersmith until appointed to the delegation that went to Breda to invite King Charles II to return to London in 1660.

On your right stand the Riverside Studios, bastion of the arts for this part of London. It occupies an old factory site, converted to film studios before its current use.

Turn right at the end, into Chancellor's Road.

The name commemorates a sub-manor of Fulham here, held by the chancellor of St Paul's Cathedral. Along the far side of the road ran its boundary ditch, 'Parr's Ditch' which carried the brook from Acton through Brook Green. Parr's Ditch is in medieval records as 'le Perre', so there was probably once a pear orchard here. A manor record of 1457 notes that 'Richard Burton is a common trespasser in the Perys croft with his geese.'

Fifty metres *before* the riverbank, turn left along the footpath.

Brandenburgh House once stood here. Originally it was Crisp's pile, 'situated in sweet and wholesome air, built very lofty, regular and magnificent after the modern manner of brick, covered with stone, with a handsome cupola at top.' After his death the house was repeatedly altered. In 1792 the occupier built a theatre in the manner of a gothic folly, the picturesque romanticism of Strawberry Hill having now percolated into national taste. The house was briefly home to the estranged Queen Caroline of Brunswick. Having been cajoled into exile in 1814, she returned on the death of George III in 1820 to claim her place as King's Consort. George IV and his advisers were not amused. Locally people rallied to her support, but her project fell apart when she was refused admittance to George's coronation at the actual doors of Westminster Abbey. Within a week she was dead: the stress and humiliation had been too great.

Brandenburgh House, with its gothic theatre on the left, c.1800.

Following her death the building was razed. A distillery was built on one part of the estate, and a sugar refinery on another.

As you walk. Intermittently along the riverbank there are traces of the wharves and moorings that once lined the riverbank. There were a variety of industrial ventures here including a jam factory (the sugar refinery was handy) and a paper works. Almost all the riverbank to Fulham was industrial or mercantile until the 1950s.

The building with rectangular white tubular steel balconies jutting out from the flank walls is Thames Reach, a Richard Rogers Partnership structure. It was built in the mid-1980s on Dorset Wharf, previously used by Duckham's Oil.

Beyond, standing back, is Thames Wharf, once another depot for lubricating oil.

From the mid-eighteenth century there was an estate here with a river frontage of about 100 metres. It was known as Dorset Cottage

The Crabtree Brewery, seen from the river c. 1890.

and it became the home of a vinegar manufacturer, Guy Champion, who lived here in the 1830s. You would not be taxed with this information were Guy Champion not a romantic eccentric:

> 'On one occasion he made a bet that he would ride a certain black horse round Europe. He left England and reached Albania. Here he chanced to attend a slave market. A lovely white girl, in nature's beauty unadorned, was offered to eager competitors. Guy bid for her and bought her. Such, however, was the influence exercised by the purchased damsel upon her purchaser that he forgot all about his bet and his ride, came back to England and married the girl.'

It was here, presumably, that he brought her. It was characteristic of his romanticism that he was so grief stricken by his brother's death that he promptly followed his example a few days later, slain by a broken heart, in 1846. Dorset Cottage with its three acres was sold off in 1876.

Turn left when you must and then right along Rainville and Holyport Roads.

The Crabtree Inn, 1895, with the brewery behind.

You are now in Crabtree. Crabtree was a hamlet in the seventeenth century with its own farmland and in due course its own inn. The present *Crabtree Inn* is on your right. It was rebuilt in the late nineteenth century. It once had far greater charm, but was progressively surrounded by malt houses at the end of the eighteenth century and then other industrial ventures. The inn served those working in the orchards on the inland side and basket makers in the osier beds along the riverside. If you hanker for this pre-industrial world, at least be thankful that the road bridge proposed here in 1928 to take a new arterial route across the river from Talgarth Road never materialised.

Turn right, under the metal pergola, straight after the inn. If you miss it, turn right down Crabtree Lane, another 50 metres further on. Follow Adam Walk back to the riverbank and continue downstream.

Newcastle Coal and Shipping Co. (est. 1933) at Rosebank Wharf, c. 1950.

At the end of Crabtree Lane stood Rosebank, in Disraeli's words 'the prettiest house in the world; a pavilion rather than a villa; all green paint, white chintz, and looking glass.' But the wooden structure burnt down in 1864.

A wharf was built and Rosebank became associated with work rather than pleasure. In 1933 the Newcastle Coal & Shipping Co. took over the wharf. It supplied the coal merchants of west London. Offloading from barges became fully mechanised in 1947. But in December 1952 London endured the densest week of smog since 1873, with smoke and sulphur dioxide levels tenfold above the normal. The Great Smog lasted less than a week but at least 1,600 and possibly twice that number of people died, principally from respiratory crises. Something had to be done. The 1956 Clean Air Act spelt the death knoll of domestic coal consumption and in 1966 the coal wharf here closed.

A few yards further downstream lay Rowberry, or Rubery Mead, which once boasted a cherry orchard 'reputed to be the finest in England'. Like much of the riverbank here, osier growing and basket making was the principal business. Rowberry is Anglo-Saxon for a rough fortified settlement, so it was an old name, now lost.

Rowberry Mead, with osier bundles drying, c.1880.

On your left are pieces of the derrick, winch and windlass machinery that once stood along here. You will notice how sensitive to its environment housing along this stretch has been.

Turn left when forced to by Fulham Football Club and right, along Stevenage Road.

One must be pretty keen on footie not to weep at the loss of Craven Cottage, which stood among the osier beds and flood meadows. How wonderful it would have been if a margin, back as far as Stevenage Road, had been left as flood meadow. Craven Cottage had been built by Elizabeth, Lady Craven, c.1780, as a *ferme ornée* (see p.98). Elizabeth, a well-regarded playwright in her day, appointed herself, one might say, as milkmaid to the courts of Europe, building *fermes ornées* on the Continent too. As one wit commented, 'everywhere that Lady Craven went, cows were sure to follow.' By the time of her death Craven Cottage internally was

Craven Cottage, c.1880.

a confection of Egyptian, Turkish and Gothic styles, 'very *recherché*' as one visitor reported.

As for Fulham Football Club, its frontage certainly has style. It was designed by Archibald Leitch, a Glaswegian specialising in such buildings, in 1905. The name Craven Cottage is preserved in the office building he also designed, set at an angle on Stevenage Road, at the downstream end of the stadium.

Turn right into Bishop's Park at the first opportunity and make your way back to the riverbank.

The embankment was built in the nineteenth century but before then there was a large shingle beach here at low water where children

Children playing in Bishop's Park, c.1900. The sand was probably brought from Margate. It was called 'Margate Sands'.

used once to frolic: a delight for the toes, thrown away by the need to shun a polluted river and by a growing obsession with embankment.

When you reach the kink in the promenade (with steps descending to the river), turn left and make for Fulham Palace.

Before entering the palace grounds it is worth knowing a little about it and you may like to find a seat. As the sketch map shows, the grounds were surrounded by a moat, regrettably filled in, 1921-24. How old the moat was remains a matter for conjecture. There is evidence of Neolithic and Iron Age occupation here. But the moat became associated with a party of Danes who supposedly wintered in Fulham in 879-880, as *The Anglo-Saxon Chronicle* records:

> '[In 879] a gang of Vikings gathered and occupied Fulham by the Thames. The same year the sun darkened for one hour of a

day. [In 880] the force that had stayed at Fulham went over the sea to Frankland, to Ghent, and stayed there for a year.'

It is unlikely the Danes dug the moat, for this would have taken most of the winter. Why would they go to that trouble if they planned to leave in the spring? They probably seized a defensible Saxon site. The moat may be pre-Saxon.

Like Putney across the river, Fulham occupies one of very few stretches on the river west of London where there is firm sand and gravel on *both* sides of the river. From Neolithic times there seems to have been a ford here. In Roman times there were settlements either side of the river. The logic is that a road forded the river here, since in those days the river was both much wider and shallower and also barely tidal.

A second critical factor is that there were streams running into the Thames on either side of the present palace grounds, along the course of Bishop's Avenue and Fulham High Street respectively. Until the river steps were built there was a river creek here, probably once the mouth of a stream. In short, the grounds formed an island of firm sand and gravel, an irresistibly good location for prehistoric settlement. These streams must have been scoured out to make the moat. On Rocque's map (see endpaper) the ground is marked 'The Eights', a misunderstanding of 'the Aits', a name presumably still in use, centuries after it had ceased to be an island. Until it was destroyed less than a century ago, the moat was over a mile in length, the longest in Britain.

The manor of Fulham was granted to the bishops of London in c.704 and the manor house only made over to the local authority in 1973, after tenure of over 1,200 years. Over the centuries buildings have been erected, adapted, demolished or replaced. Early buildings may have been on the present playgroup site near the lodge.

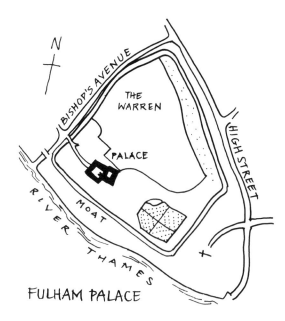

FULHAM PALACE

Enter the grounds.

The two gothic stone pillars once flanked a bridge over the moat.
The porter's lodge on the left was built c.1820 in what one might
describe as almost 'gingerbread' gothic, a romantic flight to heavy
ornamentation after the plainness, proportion and symmetry of
Regency building. On the right stands the coachman's lodge
designed in 1893 by William Butterfield, who had already built a
new chapel (see below).

The Palace

As you enter the courtyard, note **the wooden gates**. These gates
predate all the buildings now standing and have almost certainly
been salvaged from a preceding construction. The only parallel to
these gates are those for the entrance to the precinct of Peterborough

Fulham Palace: the eighteenth century development by Stiff Leadbetter.

Cathedral, and which date from the twelfth century. So as gates go, they are old.

The courtyard is early Tudor, but the buildings here were erected at different times. The older brickwork is classically Tudor with the usual diaper pattern of heavily glazed purple brick. The oldest part is the Great Hall to the left of the gateway opposite which dates from c.1480, so it just predates the Tudor period. Remodelled internally in the eighteenth century, the Great Hall's timber roof is now hidden by a plaster ceiling.

The gate tower opposite contains its original lower oriel window, the upper one being a 1920s reconstruction. All the ranges around the courtyard have been repaired, with some windows replaced at various junctures. The bell turret is eighteenth century.

Turn about and make your way to your right, around the side of the palace complex.

The museum is housed in the eighteenth century and early nineteenth century buildings that constitute the rear courtyard. It merits a visit. The rear buildings of the palace are essentially Georgian. The three principal ranges around the rear courtyard, which replaced derelict Tudor buildings, were designed by the improbably named Stiff Leadbetter. The bishop of the day had been vicar of St Mary's Twickenham and had fallen for Walpole's gothic fantasy at Strawberry Hill. So Leadbetter gave him Georgian gothic, corner towers, castellation, and arched windows for the chapel. The castellation disappeared and the frontages were much altered in 1814, as the repaired brickwork and the illustration both show.

Continue around to the back: take a seat facing the rear lawn.

Fulham Palace has an unsavoury record for brutality. Before Henry VIII had discovered how useful were the shortcomings of the Church of Rome, his prelates dealt ruthlessly with doctrinal dissidents. Torture happened here, burnings in the City.

Then came the Marian persecution. Among the many tortured here by Edmund Bonner, Bishop of London, was a weaver called Tomkins, of Shoreditch. Having failed to break Tomkins by beating, Bonner decided to persuade him to recant from his doctrinal error by holding his fingers over a fire:

> 'In which burning he never shrunk till the veins shrunk, the sinews burst, and water did spurt in [Dean] Harpsfield's face, insomuch that Harpsfield desired the bishop to stay, saying he had tried him enough. This burning was in the hall in Fulham and Boner, not contented with burning his hand, rested not until he had consumed his whole body into ashes.'

We know of these frightful events through John Foxe's *Book of Martyrs* (1563), a very Protestant account of the persecution. One might doubt the words of the martyrs as reported by Foxe until one thinks outside our liberal culture to the valedictory remarks of, say, suicide bombers. Those hoping for paradise but fearing perdition may be willing to undergo terrible adversities. An ardent Protestant Foxe may have been, but he held no hatred for those of other persuasion. He risked the wrath of Elizabeth I, frankly telling her she should spare the lives of Anabaptists condemned to death in 1575 and, more brazenly, six years later the lives of some condemned Jesuits. Foxe demands our admiration. Early in his career he wrote:

> 'We judge wrongdoers too harshly and forget the charity of the gospel. Though we hate the vice we should not hate the men.'

Four centuries later we still struggle to emulate the saintly Foxe, who must have quietly rejoiced that after Mary's death Bonner was neither tortured nor executed but simply imprisoned for his terrible deeds.

Life at Fulham Palace could still be startling in the twentieth century. One rowing blue recalled in his autobiography a lunch at the Palace in 1921 hosted by the then Bishop of London. The Oxford crew were ushered into the episcopal presence and:

> 'suddenly there he was, standing with what I believe in ecclesiastical circles is known as a Canterbury cap on his head, in a sort of somewhat claustrophobic cul-de-sac. He advanced with outstretched arms and bonhomie, saying "Boys, boys, welcome to Fulham Palace. I had better tell you right away that I have a number of curates and their wives to meet you. So you'll have a lady and a curate each. Next week I have the Cambridge crew coming. I have five bishops for them. I should think they'll have a fit." Pat Malham said, "Please, Bishop, do you think I could dispense with my curate and have two ladies?" '

G.O. Nickalls, *A Rainbow in the Sky* (1974).

The Garden

Several bishops built up the botanical collection at Fulham. Edmund Grindal started it in the mid-sixteenth century. His sole surviving legacy is a holm oak, the first to be introduced to England. In the late seventeenth century the greatest of all the collectors, arguably on a par with the other great collectors at Kew, was Henry Compton, of strongly Protestant persuasion and therefore suspended by his Catholic sovereign, James II. So, denied access to his flock, he concentrated on horticulture in collaboration with George London, a leading gardener of his day. His collection relied heavily on North American species, since he retained his diocesan responsibilities there and shrewdly despatched ministers who shared his devotion to botany and built his network of collector-contacts.

Beyond the yew hedge on your far left lie allotments, here since 1919. This was once the Warren, a game park, probably for deer, fowl and possibly also with a rabbit warren. Its principal claim on your interest is the extremely rare Turner's Oak (see below).

To your front on the far side of the lawn lies a Tudor walled garden with its own herb garden. On the right of the gate (probably locked) there are three filled-in niches in the brickwork. These are Tudor bee-boles, recesses for a hive or 'skep.' The skep is an inverted straw or rush basket inside which the bees build their comb.

Until the mid-eighteenth century, the lawn area was divided into different rectangular sections with *parterres* and the more formal planting that preceded the landscape movement. But already this was changing, for a succession of bishops were keen collectors of exotic species. Many of these exotics disappeared early on, but for arboreal enthusiasts the following sketch map indicates some 26 varieties of trees (but I have skipped some of the ones commonly found in Kew Gardens).

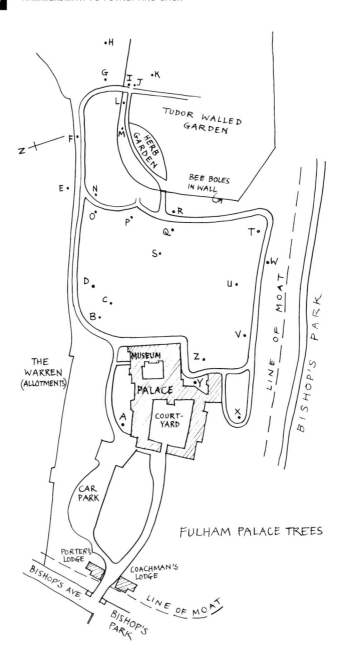

A **Cypress** or **fastigiate oak** (branches growing upwards) variety of the common English oak (*Quercus robur*), occurring naturally in central Europe. Its name is obvious once you look at the shape.

B **Black Walnut** (*Juglans nigra*) from North America, pre-1656. A finer example stands in the grounds of Marble Hill, Twickenham.

C **Judas Tree** (*Cercis siliquastrum*), lurking in the remains of a flowerbed and rather brutally lopped, a native of southern Europe and west Asia, in England by 1600, fairly common in parks and gardens.

D **Giant Redwood** (*Sequoia gigantea*) introduced from California, 1853. Can live for up to 3,400 years and reach 100m.

E **Turner's Oak**, probably c.1750, a hybrid of the common (*Q. robur*) and holm (*Q. ilex*) oak by the nurseryman Spencer Turner. It stands just beyond the yew hedge, in the Warren. Extremely rare, until very recently there were only five or six firm sightings in Western Europe, only one other in Britain, in Holland Park. Recent discussion has led to one or two more being identified. Its more holm-inclined leaves tend to over-winter.

F **Coast Redwood** (*Sequoia sempervirens*), from California, to England, 1843. On wet ground it can grow to 30m in 30 years. One in California is 112m, the tallest tree in the world. Can live over 1,000 years, rarely over 2,000 years.

G **Japanese Quince** or **japonica** (*Chaenomeles speciosa*), native of Japan and China, closely related to the true quince (*Cydonia oblonga*), characterised by its spines which the true quince does not possess.

H **Fulham Oak** (*Q. x hispanica* 'Fulhamensis'), an eighteenth century hybrid of the cork and holm oaks, evolved here at the back of the garden, hardly any anywhere else. Leaves oval and evergreen, uniformly six-toothed each side.

I **Lodgepole pine** (*Pinus contorta latifolia*) was only introduced from America in 1854. It acquired its name on account of its use as a tepee pole. It remains rare in Britain.

J **Medlar** (*Mespilus germanica*) possibly originating in southern Europe, this tree was in England by the fourteenth century, Chaucer describing how the fruit had to be bletted (left once picked to go over-ripe) to be edible. It was a popular Victorian dessert, and remains the perfect accompaniment to Scotch.

K **Norway spruce** (*Picea abies*) grows all over north Europe and Russia, introduced into England by 1500.

L **Clerodendrum** (*Clerodendrum mexicanum)* As its name implies, from Central America.

M **Mimosa** (*Acacia dealbata*) brought from Australia, c.1820, now quite common.

N **Pride of India** or **Golden Rain** (*Keulreutaria paniculata*), actually from the Far East (China-Japan), mid-eighteenth century.

O **Yellow Wood** (*Cladastris lutea*) introduced from Eastern USA in 1812, and rare here.

P **Tupelo** or **Black Gum** (*Nyssa sylvatica*) introduced from NE America before 1750.

Q **Dawn Redwood** or **Water fir** (*Metasequoia glyptostroboides*) only discovered in 1941 in south-west China, introduced to Britain in 1948.

R **Maidenhead** (*Ginko biloba*), introduced from China in 1758, a very ancient tree dating back to the Jurassic period.

S **Strawberry Tree** (*Arbutus unedo*), in the flowerbed, a native of western Ireland with an edible but unpalatable fruit, hence *unedo* ('I eat [only] one'). It is evergreen, with ascending sinuous branches and a rounded low head.

T **Holm oak** (*Quercus ilex*) one of many in the grounds, this particular tree probably dates back to circa 1500, the first in Britain and the only surviving tree from the garden laid out by Grindal. Its central trunk has now disappeared, and it grows out of the peripheral roots. It is a native of Italy and other southern European lands. It may have been planted deliberately, but possibly not. For it was at about this time that the magnate class in England first started collecting Italian cultural artefacts. Acorns of the holm oak were used as packing material, the polystyrene of its day, so the frequency and apparent popularity of holm oaks in the gardens of great houses may be initially explained by reckless dumping of refuse, rather than deliberate arboriculture.

U **Indian Bean Tree** (*Catalpa bignioides*) introduced in 1726 from south-eastern USA, distinguished by its long seed pods. It stands close to a leaning black mulberry tree, but is immediately distinguishable by its long seed pods.

V **Amur Maple** (*Acer ginnala*): from China c.1860.

W **Bhutan Pine** (*Pinus wallachiana*), grows naturally between Afghanistan and Nepal, introduced to Britain, 1823, now quite common.

X **Tulip Tree** (*Liriodendron tulipifera*) from south-east and mid-west US, introduced to Britain in 1650.

Having admired the tulip tree, note the original Tudor bargeboards on the gables on your right. And to the right of them, the William Butterfield chapel built in 1866. Butterfield is better known for his work for the Tractarian movement, with which he became identified: most notably, All Saints, Margaret Street, London (1859), and Keble College, Oxford (1876). Butterfield had an original style, his principal decorative characteristics were polychromy, diapered and striped brickwork. In the 1960s a wag chalked on Keble College wall: 'Not so much a Collage, more a Fair Isle sweater.' Here his work is more restrained, but not restrained enough for 1950s taste. In 1953 pale murals by Brian Thomas masked the patterned brickwork of the interior. They rob the chapel of its visual integrity and jar badly with Butterfield's vision. From sweater to cardigan, one might say.

Y Paperbark Maple (*Acer griseum*) West China, introduced 1901.

Z Cork oak (*Q. suber*) late seventeenth cent, from S. Europe.

Leave the palace, cleaving to the left through the gardens between the filled-in moat on your left and the riverbank on your right.

Enter the grounds of All Saints', Fulham's church (open weekdays, 12-3pm and during service times on Sundays).

The tower is Kentish ragstone, and was built in the 1440s. If it looks familiar, it is. This Thames valley style is typical for the period. The tower is home to a peal of ten bells in the key of E. The rest of the church was rebuilt by Arthur Blomfield, son of a bishop of London in the 1880s, a faithfully scaled late Perpendicular church. If you can, go inside. There is a guide to some remarkable memorials and the beautiful altar reredos. Look out for William Payne, 1626, in the south chapel, on the right of the nave. Payne bequeathed 'an Ilande in the river Thames caled Makenshawe to the use of the poore of this Parish on Hamersmyth side'. The island in question became a portion of the largest and lowest of the 'Brentford' aits, just above Kew Bridge.

Outside, the churchyard appears orderly but was once used to misbehaviour. In 1611 the inhabitants of Fulham street were all fined because they 'suffered their hoggs and hoggerells to come and go into the churchyard.' The churchyard has become a stranger to hoggerells since then.

Make your way to the main road and turn right onto the bridge.

The first bridge was built in 1729, completely out of oak, which proved its worth by outlasting two subsequent stone bridges, at Westminster and Blackfriars respectively. Oak minds the wet a lot less than most timber. It simply requires periodic piecemeal refurbishment. The bridge was built at breakneck speed, eight months in all.

Fulham Bridge was still in good condition when it was finally freed of tolls in 1880. By then virtually all the fields had gone, replaced by bricks and mortar, and the population increased about twenty fold. The removal of tolls led to a substantial increase in traffic and it was this increase that brought the bridge to a dangerously stressed condition. It had started life as a country bridge and simply could not stand the rigours of an urban environment.

Fulham Bridge had made its way across the river at an angle about twenty paces downstream of the present Putney Bridge. An awkward curve brought the bridge around the foreshore in front of the church to link with Putney High Street. The new bridge built between 1882 and 1886, runs straight to Putney High Street from a new approach road off Fulham High Street. The present bridge in fact followed the course of an aqueduct built in 1852 to convey the Chelsea Waterworks' water to its subscribers from reservoirs on Putney Heath after it was required by law to take up its water from above the tidal head, effectively above Kingston.

Fulham Bridge and the aqueduct that was replaced by Putney Bridge.

The Surrey bank.

As you approach the Surrey bank, avert your gaze from the Tower of Babel lowering over St Mary's Church. If you care either about architecture or about democracy, then St Mary's, not its bullying neighbour, is definitely worth a visit, so check if it is open. (If you wish to skip it, turn to p.205.) The most important architectural feature is the late medieval chantry chapel, built by a Putney-born bishop of Ely who died in 1533, now at the far (east) end on the left (north) side of the nave. It is one of very few such chapels surviving in the environs of London. The medieval church was rebuilt in the mid-1830s, but gutted by fire in 1973. The interior was radically but skilfully restored by Ronald Sims.

Being an ardent democrat, you will not wish to pass on your way without recollecting how, as a result of discussion here, our parliamentary democracy might have happened more than two

centuries earlier than in fact it did. Having decisively defeated the
Royalist forces at Naseby in 1646, the Roundhead army was restive
knowing that Parliament was bankrupt but unable to dissolve it
without substantial arrears of pay. It correctly suspected Parliament
of being willing to hand back to the Crown virtually all the powers it
had enjoyed prior to the civil war. In October 1647 the Army Council
met around the communion table to listen to various political ideas
from soldiers who wanted a democratic future.

Of all the voices heard during the debate in October 1647, one in
particular rings across the centuries, that of Colonel Thomas
Rainborow. He led the republican section among those officers
opposed to further negotiation with Charles I. This is the statement
he made to the Council (and you should probably be respectfully on
your feet for this stuff):

> 'I think that the poorest he that is in England hath a life to live
> as the greatest he; and therefore truly, sir, I think it is clear
> that every man that is to live under a government ought first
> by his own consent to put himself under the government, and
> I do think that the poorest man in England is not at all bound
> in a strict sense to that government that he hath not had a
> voice to put himself under…. I do not find anything in the
> Law of God that a lord shall choose twenty burgesses, and a
> gentleman but two, or a poor man shall choose none. I find
> no such thing in the Law of Nature, nor in the Law of Nations.
> But I do find that all Englishmen must be subject to English
> laws, and I do verily believe that there is no man but will say
> that the foundation of all law lies in the people…. Every man
> born in England cannot, ought not, neither by the Law of God
> nor the Law of Nature, to be exempted from the choice of
> those who are to make laws for him to live under, and for him,
> for aught I know, to lose his life under.'

Putney High Street with an exceptionally high water in 1882. One can just see the masonry end of the aqueduct on the right.

Bravo. But preaching the fundamentals of a modern parliamentary democracy was a bad career move in the mid-seventeenth century. Generals are apt to like things neat, hierarchical and orderly and are not naturally enamoured of messy democracy. Rainborow, recently appointed vice-admiral of Parliament's fleet, was relieved of his command until he formally recanted his views and pledged obedience to Cromwell. Sadly, he did recant. In the meantime, in 1648 the king misplayed his hand and so lost his head in January 1649, and Cromwell progressively arrogated to himself the powers of a dictator and proved significantly worse than the Stuart monarchy.

Cross the road back to the riverbank upstream. Follow the right fork sloping down to the riverbank.

Immediately on your right is Putney's old draw dock, cobbled but with paved tracks to facilitate traction for horse-drawn carts. If it is low water you will see what is left of the shingle that once ran along this riverfront until it was embanked and concreted over about a century ago.

Here you enter one of rowing's hallowed spots, with the start of the Oxford and Cambridge Boat Race and a succession of boat-houses (on the Boat Race and race-rowing more generally, see p.238). There have been rowing clubs on the tideway since the mid-nineteenth century. Since then there have always been keen rowers on the Thames but most of us males prefer lazily watching. One worried commentator wrote retrospectively almost a century ago:

> 'Undoubtedly the tideway rowing clubs had a very uphill and ceaseless struggle against the forces of ease and enjoyment which had so invidiously encroached on the battleground of British manliness.'

When it comes to average British manliness today, let's face it, there has been a rout. And while more and more women are now rowing, they are a rebuke to all those females who prefer lazily watching, reinforcing the real dividing line in life which has nothing at all to do with gender. It is really between those splendid physical specimens out there on the river, and the rest of us skulking in our armchairs.

Look out for the footbridge across Beverley Brook.

Do not take the bridge for granted. There was still a watersplash in 1792 when the residents of Barnes, for whom this was still the only way to Putney, finally got fed up with arriving spattered in mud and put up money for a wooden bridge, upstream of the present bridge. Beverley Brook rises in Sutton, ambles through Richmond Park and across the southern marches of Mortlake and Barnes to debouch into the Thames here. Its name, 'beaver stream' (-ley is a corrupted version of *lacu*, Anglo Saxon for a stream) almost certainly dates from before the Conquest, for beavers became extinct in the eleventh or twelfth century.

Straight after the bridge you pass a line of Lombardy poplars. Lombardy poplars are single gene mutants of the native black poplar, the principal excitement along this stretch of riverbank.

Remains of Romano-British fish traps have been found along this stretch of the river, further evidence of Roman presence in Putney and Fulham.

Behind the trees on your left, now playing fields, once stood Barn Elms, the manor house of the whole manor of Barnes. Elizabeth I's spymaster, Francis Walsingham lived here from 1579 till his death in 1590. Walsingham was passionately and inflexibly Protestant, relentless in pursuit of Catholic conspirators. He tortured and destroyed those he caught. No soft liberal edges there.

After about 300 metres, a footpath comes in from your left.

This marks the beginning of the Barnes Wetlands Centre (see p.212), the welcome consignment to wildlife of four massive reservoirs dug out of the estate in 1894. These took water from Hampton Waterworks on the Middlesex bank upstream (see vol. 1, p.24).

The reservoirs had been dug on the site of Barn Elms farm and a house called Queen Elizabeth's Dairy. These were virtually the only other buildings apart from Barn Elms itself standing on the Barnes peninsula until Hammersmith Bridge was thrown across the river in the mid-1820s. Queen Elizabeth's Dairy acquired brief fame in the early eighteenth century as the rural retreat of the Kit-Cat Club. The members were largely leading literary figures but also the ultimate Whig politician, Robert Walpole. Their covert purpose was to secure the Protestant succession through the House of Hanover. Walsingham would have been pleased.

Barn Elms farm, the old manor farm, was leased to a number of people, among them William Cobbett from 1827-31. Cobbett was a radical, deeply committed to the rural labouring class. He grew maize here and vainly hoped to persuade the British public to abandon potatoes in favour of this alternative American import. He also grew a special straw in the hope of reviving the straw plaiting industry for the fruitful winter employment of country labourers. Cobbett was an accomplished writer. His *Grammar* (1818) was still in use in British schools a century later, not least because he cheekily quoted the infelicities of contemporary celebrities, for example George III and Wellington, to illustrate what not to write.

Stop after another 500 metres when you reach Steve Fairbairn's memorial beside the towpath.

The plaque probably says all you need to know.

Retrace your way by thirty paces. This is a mandatory pilgrimage.

You stand before a native black poplar (*populus nigra*). Native black poplars are a real rarity. There are approximately 3,000 left in England, even fewer on the Continent and less than 30 north of a line from the Wash to the Mersey. Virtually half of all England's surviving black poplars stand in the wetter parts of the Vale of Aylesbury. They are loners, seldom growing in woodland but on their own in the swampy conditions of flood plains. Their shape is characterised almost invariably by a leaning trunk with branches that sweep downwards only to turn up again. If allowed to grow on swampy ground, their proper environment, they will grow into massive and magnificent trees, in the words of Oliver Rackham, the countryside historian, 'no other native tree can compete with it in rugged grandeur.' No other tree has such deeply fissured bark, except the hybrid black and grey poplar. But the grey poplar is more

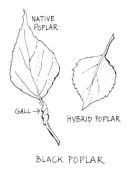

slender in shape and cannot manage such mass, while the hybrid black tends to have more regular fissures without the burrs and boles of the native (as demonstrated by the trees further upstream (see p.179)). Black poplars are either male (crimson catkins) or female (green catkins), but the female is so rare that males tend to reproduce not by cross-pollination but by falling over, a not infrequent occurrence on unstable river gravel. Fallen trunks and even branches have a knack of rooting themselves. One can mistake some hybrids for the native but there is a failsafe method of distinguishing the two when in full leaf. Virtually invariably the native is the specific host to a particular aphid, which leaves a telltale gall on the stalk of the leaf. It does the same thing with Lombardy poplars but the hybrid and the grey poplar are of no interest to the aphid and remain unaffected.

Three hundred years ago England had several times as many black poplars as today. Progressive drainage of swampy ground has reduced their favoured habitat. What a shame we do not listen to warnings against the way we impoverish ourselves:

'What would the world be, once bereft
Of wet and wildness? Let them be left,
O let them be left, wildness and wet;
Long live the weeds and the wilderness yet.'

Gerard Manley Hopkins, *Inversnaid*

So, even here, literally a stone's throw from the late Victorian reservoirs that now constitute Barnes Wetlands, we have lost the river's wildness and wet. These trees or their ancestors started life with their feet virtually in the river, on an unkempt, ragged, moist and muddy riverbank, a rich profusion little more than a century ago of orange balsam (Touch-me-not), great hairy bitter cress, mouse-eared chickweed, cow parsnip, sweet flag, frogbit, meadow-sweet and other wetland plants. But over the past two centuries we have progressively and bossily encroached and over-organised the river shallows. The soft verges are gone, and instead we have given this wonderful river the hard shoulder. Must it really be like this?

Black poplar wood is heat resistant and therefore was widely used for the floorboards of oast and malthouses. Its springy quality makes it ideal should you ever want a pair of clogs or wooden brake blocks for your haywain. The bark was frequently used by fishermen as floats for their nets. According to tradition, the black poplar provided the wood for Calvary. Its shimmering leaves remain its eternal punishment, but this cursed tree is one from which you may yet find succour. If you suffer agues or fevers, just pin a lock of your hair to the bark and recite:

> 'When Christ our Lord was on the Cross,
> Then didst thou sadly shiver and toss,
> My aches and pains thou now must take,
> Instead of me I bid thee shake.'

Struck speechless by so peerless a ditty, go straight home without uttering a word. Your cure will follow.

Back to mundane reality. If you wish to keep an eye out for the rest, another three or four black poplars await you. As you pass them, you may like to call to mind how Rackham describes them: 'the last shadow of the vanished flood plain wildwood' and, here in suburbia, feel duly privileged.

The last black poplar stands just before you reach the Harrods Depository, now converted into desirable flats. There is not much to say about the Depository, built in the 1890s, and you would probably prefer to know about the store. Charles Harrod was a wholesale tea merchant in Eastcheap. He opened a small grocer's shop in the village of Knightsbridge in 1849. His son took it over in

1861 and 20 years later he was employing over 100 shop assistants. But in December 1883, the shop burnt down. To anyone else it would have been a catastrophe. Undaunted, Harrod wrote that day to inform all his customers, apologising and saying that in consequence, 'your order will be delayed in the execution by a day or two.' Now *that* is class and his customers recognised it as such. By the time the shop was rebuilt in 1884, Harrod's turnover had more than doubled. Back to the Depository, or rather what previously stood here.

Once, this had been arable land. In 1858 a soap and candle works was established on the site. Soap and candles were both made from tallow. But in the middle years of the nineteenth century the industrial process eclipsed traditional methods. Free of tax in 1853 (see p.63 for the story of soap up to then), cleanliness came within easy reach of the poor for the first time and soap works sprang up around the country. This was one of them. By the time it closed in 1892, following a fire, scrubbing, notably the backs of boyish ears and the treads of front doorsteps, had become a national obsession.

Return to Hammersmith via the bridge.

Barnes Wetlands Centre

Website: www.wwt.org.uk
E-mail: info.London@wwt.org.uk
Tel: 020 8409 4400

The Wetlands Centre is proof, if one was needed, of the symbiotic relationship that humankind can achieve with its environment. It is the brainchild of Peter Scott, who died in 1989, and was taken up by the owner, Thames Water. The four enormous reservoirs had just been made redundant by the London ring main. Nevertheless, the wetland is still fed from water uptake at Hampton. A developer took 20 acres, providing £11 million to help create a wetland out of the remaining 105 acres. Half a million cubic metres of soil, clay and concrete were removed.

    The wetland is certainly not natural, but then nor is Kew Gardens or indeed any managed landscape. What contrived landscapes do is to offer something that cannot otherwise exist. Kew Gardens preserves exotic and rare plants. The Wetlands Centre provides a habitat for exotic birds, brought in to demonstrate the global variety of wetland fowl. More importantly it provides a haven for endangered native species, for example the lapwing. Until the 1970s the lapwing, with its iridescent green back, its black and white under-parts and long wispy crest was a common enough sight. But its numbers more than halved between 1970 and 2000. In Wales it declined by 70 per cent in the last decade of the twentieth century. They have been devastated by monoculture, with the abandonment of mixed arable-livestock farming, and intensified field drainage. Here one can enjoy lapwings with their spectacular way of tumbling out of the sky to drive off predators. Altogether there are over 150 birds and over 300 butterfly and moth species that use these wetlands yearly.

APPENDIX 1

The Thames, its banks, river craft and human activity

A GEOLOGICAL HISTORY OF THE THAMES

Eighty million years ago Britain was submerged in a sea of clear water and a layer of chalk was laid down on the seabed. This phase came to an end with the rising of the sea floor, sufficient to bring the whole of the British area above sea level, sloping in an easterly and south-easterly direction.

Sixty million years ago, during another phase of submergence for south-eastern Britain, a thick mass of marine clay was deposited. It is 300-400 ft deep with fossils of extinct mammals, birds, turtles, crocodiles and fish.

Forty million years ago a vast river flowed eastwards across the British landmass, leaving major sandbanks, in London notably the Hampstead-Highgate ridge.

Thirty million years ago the precursor of the Thames rose in the Cotswolds and flowed north-east across the Vale of Oxford. It carried at least tenfold the present quantity of water.

Between twenty and five million years ago earth movements created folds in the chalk underlying the London Clay, resulting in the creation of the London Basin, with the Chilterns to the north and the North Downs on the south side.

Two million years ago, during the ice age, glacial ice cut the Goring Gap through the hills near Maidenhead, creating a new river route. This forerunner of the Thames flowed eastwards between the two chalk slopes, across the Vale of St Albans and into the forerunner of the Rhine in the southern area of the present North Sea. It was during the folding phase that water became trapped between the chalk folds and the clay on top of it, thus creating London's artesian wells.

During the Great Ice Age, which set in about 500,000 years ago, all Britain north of Watford was under glacier. The course of the river was now unable to run through the Vale of St Albans into East Anglia. The present course was adopted only after the advancing ice cap forced the river southwards 450,000 years ago. During the following 200,000 years or so there were repeated phases of glaciation and thaw. During the thaw the river would probably have been a torrent carrying many times its present flow, dropping the largest pieces of mineral debris soonest, the finer gravels and pebbles further downstream.

The melt phases greatly increased the strength of the river, thereby cutting a progressively deeper channel. These left three major terraces, at different levels representing the outflow of successive ice sheets. The highest and oldest is the 'Boyn Hill' terrace, about 400,000 years old and mainly about 100 feet above the river, then the 'Taplow' terrace, about 150,000 years old and 50 feet above the river; and the most recent flood plain, about 15,000 years old and 25 feet above the river. That said, there are local variations and landslip that make the terraces difficult to identify in places. The oldest river gravels and flood loams are thickest and most extensive in ill-defined terraces at varying elevations easily observable between Walton and Petersham, Richmond and Wandsworth. High terraces are formed on Kingston Hill, Wimbledon Common, Richmond Hill and Putney Heath.

By 8000BC the southern part of the North Sea was still a swampy tract and was only finally submerged at the present Straits of Dover in about 6000BC. Many places along the river covered in gravel, loam, wind-borne loess or brick-earth, are of relatively recent origin. The shape of the river has changed over the millenia too. Every bend in the meandering river has been slowly moving downstream as it erodes the outer curve and drops deposits on the inner one, sometimes resulting in an oxbow lake. In other words, the exact course of the river has been constantly changed by its own kinetic effect.

There were once hundreds of small islands and marshy areas along the flat valley floor. Some of these still survive, often called 'aits' or 'eyots', a word derived from the Anglo-Saxon. Most of these have disappeared, reclaimed into the riverbank by human activity. During the past two millennia it is human intervention which has had the most significant impact on the character of the river.

THE TIDE

Tides result from the gravitational pull mainly of the moon but also of the sun. The earth and moon rotate once every 28-day (lunar) month, creating an oceanic bulge on the side facing the moon and a centrifugal force raising a similar bulge on the reverse side of the earth. The earth rotates beneath these oceanic bulges, creating the daily rise and fall of tide, two high and two low waters every 24 hours (to be pedantic there is a slight time lag, the whole tidal sequence taking 24 hours and 50 minutes). The tides also follow a 28-day cycle reflecting changes in the alignment of earth, moon and sun. The largest gravitational pull is when the sun and moon are in line, producing 'spring' tides. When the sun and moon are at right angles, a weaker 'neap' tide occurs with a reduced range between high and low water. Additional variations occur because of the elliptical orbits of earth and moon. When the moon and the earth are closest, the tides are 20 per cent greater. Spring tides are already 30 per cent greater than neap tides.

How does the river estuary affect the tide? The tidal surge is greater in an estuary than out at sea and there is a time lag between high water at sea and up the estuary. The stronger 'spring' tides are usually in the afternoon, while 'neap' tides are normally morning tides.

The land has been slowly sinking over the centuries. When the Romans invaded, the Thames at London was possibly still not perceptibly tidal. Since then high water levels have been increasing at a rate of 70 cm per century. The construction of London Bridge in the early Middle Ages reduced tidal impact, penning water back but also reducing the effect of incoming tides. It also reduced the flow and the salinity. One consequence was that the river froze more easily. In the seventeenth century London Bridge seems to have limited the effective range of the tide to Molesey. The medieval bridge was not replaced until 1831, by which time locks and weirs had reduced the tidal impact above Teddington. The river was bordered largely by flood meadows to cope with high water. Today no fewer than 1 ¼ million people in London work below the average high water level.

The immediate cause of the highest water levels is a strong spring tide combined with a 'surge' tide. Surge tides are due to zones of low pressure off the Canadian coast, beneath which the sea rises approximately 30 cm over an area up to 1,000 miles across. Normally such 'humps' of water cross the Atlantic at about 50 mph passing north of Britain. A strong northerly wind will push the hump into the North Sea where, because of the narrowness of the Straits of Dover, water is funnelled up the Thames Estuary. If combined with an unusually heavy river outflow following a sustained period of rainfall, the risk of flooding is obviously increased. It was for this that the Thames Barrier was constructed 1974-82. By February 2004 it had been raised 88 times. The incidence of closing the Barrier is increasing, as is inundation of the towpath. The Barrier is still expected to last its predicted effective life to 2030. Yet the apparently increased incidence of low-pressure zones and attendant Atlantic surges must raise questions about climate change.

Campshedding, revetments and embankments on the Thames have made the river flow faster than ever before. They have also increased the differential between high and low water, which now ranges between four and seven metres. In the past the loss of flood meadows and the creation of campshedding increased the outflow of water. Climate change, with more frequent heavy rainstorms, is expected to lead to a 20 per cent increase in the quantity of water passing Teddington Weir. This raises a major question regarding the critical section where outflow meets the tidal head, between Teddington and Richmond locks. Eight major flood barriers on Thames tributaries have been built to assist control the outflow. How effective will they be in future? Without the Thames Barrier, there have been recent occasions when water would have been 1 ½ metres higher, causing very extensive damage. In theory 400,000 London properties are at risk in a 45 square mile area that would flood were it not for flood defences. Ham Lands, or part of these lands, may be returned to flood meadow. In principle, this would be sound river management and sound environmental ecology.

The Thames is currently entirely fresh above Battersea. The water repeatedly sloshes to and fro with the tide. Overall, its progress to the sea is little more than two miles per day. At high and low water, the river is 'slack', and the tidal ebb and flow reach maximum speed exactly midway between high and low water.

EARLY HOMINID AND HUMAN HABITATION

Paleolithic implements have been found at East Sheen and Battersea Rise, indicating human presence 12,000 years ago, but actual colonisation happened probably in the Mesolithic or Neolithic periods, between 8000 and 2000BC. This meant clearing woodland and creating grassland and flood meadow in place of swampy woodland. One result was the spread of fritillaries right along all the flood meadows of the Thames. Progressive draining more or less eliminated them.

The river remained the best means of travel from Neolithic times until the advent of turn-pike (toll-maintained) roads in the mid-eighteenth century. Goods continued to travel more efficiently by water until the advent of rail in the mid-nineteenth century.

The river has become increasingly curvaceous over the centuries. The water tends to drop its silt on the inside of the bend, while washing the silt off the outer bend to leave the gravel bed exposed. As a consequence almost all the oldest settlements lie on these outside curves. Think, for example, of Barnes, a village tucked into the outside curve, leaving the whole of the Barnes peninsula as osier beds, flood meadow and pasture for many centuries. Barnes peninsula was only really colonised in the nineteenth century. There are one or two exceptions to this rule, notably Fulham, opposite Putney, because it has gravel.

REGULATING THE RIVER: AUTHORITY, LOCKS AND WEIRS

The more traditional purpose of weirs was to channel the flow of water for milling, although this was more easily arranged on Thames tributaries, and to catch fish (see p.224). The earliest known navigational weirs were 'flash' weirs, made of two rows of timber stakes and brushwood 'hedges' in-filled with chalk, turf or stones. They would be constructed with a removable section of sluices up to 6 metres wide, to allow the passage of barges. The moveable pieces, 'paddles', probably oak, rested against posts known as 'rymers' and were held in place by the pressure of the water. It is to this moveable part that the term 'lock' originally referred. Opening the lock invariably caused a massive loss of water, perhaps a fall of 30 cm over a three mile stretch of river. From Richmond downstream the river was simply too wide for locks.

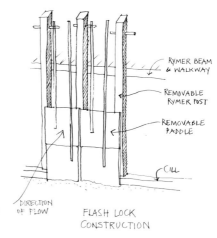

RYMER BEAM & WALKWAY

REMOVABLE RYMER POST

REMOVABLE PADDLE

CILL

DIRECTION OF FLOW

FLASH LOCK CONSTRUCTION

In certain places 'half-weirs' were used, primarily for navigation, simply to divert the flow and increase the water depth in otherwise shallow channels. For example, they were often sited between an ait (island) and the river-bank, to increase the flow between the ait and the opposite bank.

Keeping the river open for navigation was a constant preoccupation for the authorities. In 1197 Richard I sold the rights to the River Thames (but not the river bed) to the Corporation of the City of London to raise money for his Crusade. This charter 'commanded that all weirs that are in the Thames be removed.... For it is manifest to us ... that great detriment and inconvenience hath grown to our said City of London... by occasion of the said weirs.' Clause 23 of Magna Carta, 1215, also required the demolition of all fish-trap weirs. Until the eighteenth century there were repeated orders for clearing the river of navigational hazards, of which fish-weirs seem to have been the greatest nuisance. Fisher-men encroached again as soon as the authorities were less vigilant.

It was only in the latter part of the eighteenth century, that steps were taken to ensure proper navigation of the Thames. The Thames Navigation Commissioners were given powers in 1770, by which time the construction of canals had made unobstructed navigation an imperative. The Commissioners were authorised to acquire land by compulsory purchase: for the construction and maintenance of towpaths, as horses began to displace halers (see *towing*, p.229) and to buy old flash locks and weirs and 'to erect and maintain pounds or turnpikes where locks or weirs are now made use of.' These 'pound' or 'cistern' locks were essentially what we have now.

EMBANKMENT OF THE RIVER

Wood was the first material used to define the riverbank. Particularly good timbers for river work were the alder and elm, both of which remain extremely durable if never dried. Shoring up the sides of the river became known as 'campshedding', almost certainly a corruption of the Dutch word *kant-schot*, translated as 'sideboard' or 'curb'. Dutchmen were employed because of the great skill they acquired with their canals and drainage works.

THAMES POLLUTION, HEALTH AND WATERWORKS

Estimated London population in

1500	50,000
1600	200,000
1700	650,000
1800	900,000
1850	2,000,000
1900	5,000,000

One may safely assume that people have routinely thrown filth into the Thames since earliest times. The flow conveniently carries it out of sight. By Tudor times salmon, gudgeon, shrimp dace, roach and lamprey were still quite common. But it was then, with the dramatic expansion of London, that the river started to deteriorate. The head-waters of the River Fleet in Hampstead and Highgate were tapped by 1550, and the River Lea by the early seventeenth century. Lower down the Fleet the story was different. Ben Jonson, describing a boat journey at that time up the Fleet, observed the seat of every privy 'fill'd with buttock and the walls do sweat urine and plaisters....' while every oar stroke 'belch'd forth an ayre as hot as the muster of all your night-tubs.' A century later, while human excrement remained the chief pollutant, there was also the waste of 150 city slaughter houses, the fish market, tanneries as well as domestic rubbish. By 1828 at least 140 sewers discharged into the Thames. In addition the ground water of London became heavily polluted, because of the increasing use of cesspits for human waste and the demise of the 'night-soil' trade, which removed human excreta by cart from the city. During the 1830s and 1840s the newfangled flush lavatory made things much worse, with a rapidly increasing quantity of untreated sewage pouring into the river from which many still drew water to drink.

Cholera provided the impetus to do something. It had appeared in India in 1818 and made its way westwards. London's first cholera epidemic killed 5,000 in February 1832. The 1849 cholera outbreak claimed 14,000 Londoners. Consequently the 1852 Metropolitan Water Act made it illegal to draw drinking water from the tidal Thames with effect from 1855. There was therefore a rush by the private water companies to identify sites as close to Teddington lock as possible. The new waterwork sites included pump houses and filter beds. Water passed through the filter beds (described below), and was then pumped into the distributive system using coal-fired engines. The virtue of clean water was proven by the 1849 outbreak. While the Southwark & Vauxhall Water Company was still drawing water for consumption at Battersea, the Lambeth Company were already in compliance with the new law, taking its water at Thames Ditton. The former had a death rate among its clients of 130 per 10,000. The Lambeth company, which had previously had a similar death rate, could now claim a rate of only 37 per 10,000. It was also noted that the Chelsea Waterworks Company had been providing utterly safe water since 1829 through a method called 'slow sand filtration', developed by a Paisley engineer, James Simpson. This method passed water through different gradations of sand, gravel and bricks which both filtered out particles physically and destroyed bacteria bio-chemically. It became universally applied, saving literally millions of lives. Simpson remains the great unsung hero of urban public health.

CLEANING UP THE RIVER

The first imperative was to remove London's sewage, achieved through Joseph Bazalgette's astonishing network of sewers, 1858-1875, which is still in use today. His system was capable of handling 400 million gallons of waste daily. The outflow was sited at Barking Creek, safely downstream of London, or so it was thought. However, the tidal flow brought some of it up again, thus still leaving the lower river extremely unsavoury even after the 1887 separation of solid and liquid waste with the former dumped out at sea.

However, gas works were sited close to the river to facilitate delivery and off-loading of coal and the river became a natural recipient of its highly polluting unwanted by-products, ammonia liquor and carbolic acid. By 1850 the tidal river was effectively dead and remained so between Hammersmith and Gravesend for a century. In 1957 there was still no fish life in the London Thames.

A major effort was then made to clean the river. By 1963 eels, a pretty hardy lot, had reappeared. In the early 1970s there were bream, roach, dace and flounder. By the end of the decade perch, pike, sprat, goby, brown and rainbow trout and stickleback were to be found. In the 1990s bass, bullhead, carp and salmon came back too. By 2000, 118 species of fish had returned to the estuary. The London Thames is regularly re-oxygenated if levels fall sufficiently to threaten aquatic life, for example when sudden downpours lead to a major influx of water with rotting matter from London's drains.

Yet the vulnerability of river life was demonstrated in August 2004 when the stress on the drainage and sewage system led Thames Water to discharge 650,000 tons of effluent from the Mogden sewage works, between Twickenham and Isleworth. It is estimated that about 100,000 fish, principally carp, chub, bream, dace, tench as well as lamprey, died as a consequence of the sudden drop in oxygen levels. It has been proposed to construct a 22-mile sewage pipe to carry treated effluent well downstream of London. It would cost an estimated £26 billion. A clean river does not come cheap.

HARVESTING THE RIVER BANKS

Osier growing and basket making. The osier is a willow bush (*Salix viminalis*), very fast growing with straight shoots and used for wickerwork. The osier industry was seasonal, and could take place during slack times in agriculture or fishing. Most of the aits on the Thames were devoted to osier beds (see p.163). Osiers are grown in beds locally known as 'twig aits' or 'twig hawes'. Rods are graded according to their designated purpose and dried. When they are to be used, the bundles are immersed in hot water or in steam for stripping the bark. Osiers were used for almost any kind of container possible: eelbucks and crayfish pots, baskets for livestock or crops; laundry or bread baskets.

The crack willow tree, or *Salix fragilis*, grows so fast it is apt to split open under its own weight. It likes damp or boggy places. It is often planted along riverbanks to help stabilise them. Each tree is customarily pollarded every six or seven years, to prevent the weight of growth splitting the tree open and because by this time the shoots have reached the right size to make strong but springy poles. Willow wands often root, sometimes wholly unintentionally. Wands are still used to support the riverbank, as well as bridge footings, hurdles, furniture and wattle in housing construction.

FISH, FISHING AND FISH-TRAPS

In the Middle Ages there were fisheries at Isleworth, Brentford, Strand-on-the-Green, Mortlake, Fulham. Ancient stakes were found at Railshead, probably so named after these stakes or rails at the head of the fishery. Frequently caught species on the tidal reaches were sturgeon, smelt (a small relative of the salmon), salmon, eels and lamprey. Salmon remained a valuable catch. Stories of London apprentices declining salmon for dinner more than once a week are apocryphal. By 1630 the City of London introduced regulations to protect fish stocks and breeding, notably smelt, salmon and lamprey. It also decreed that bull rushes, flags and sedges should not be cut between Staines and Richmond 'for they are a great Succour and Safeguard unto the fish.' So where are they now? Embankment has done for them. It also increases the flow of water making it harder for many species to reproduce successfully.

Kiddels were fairly permanent weirs designed to create downstream shallows in which lampreys (which enjoy muddy shallows) and fish could be caught. These were screens of stakes and hurdles set across part of the current, thickly woven with bushy twigs or wickerwork.

Hoopnets made of string and weighted with triangular shaped brick weights (that can still sometimes be found on the foreshore) were used to catch the overnight upstream movement of fish.

Eelbucks faced upstream to catch eels swimming downstream overnight. Bucks were set in good current. *'Grig-weels'* were cigar-shaped traps, made of willow rods narrowing inward and baited. A 'grig' is a type of eel, and a weel another term for a buck. The eel forces its body through but the rods would spring back closing off any escape.

Crayfish and freshwater lobsters were caught in pots made from withy rods, baited and placed near their holes on the riverbed in the evening.

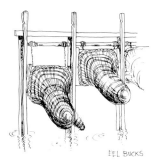

EEL BUCKS

RIVER CRAFT

The difficulty with traditional craft and their construction is that many of the technical terms mean different things at different times and in different places. No list of terms has much hope of being comprehensive unless in a book on its own. The following words and illustrations are listed in the hope of being helpful rather than confusing.

Boat construction

A few technical terms, with illustrations, of what is visible: *'Clinker'* boats are built with overlapping or 'clenched' strakes or planks, rivetted together with nails. *'Carvel'* boats are built from strakes or planks laid edge to edge, with any gaps filled with flexible caulking. Virtually all Thames boats were clinker construction, except for some very large barges and also racing rowboats: 'sculls', 'fours' and 'eights'. Plywood technology allowed racing boats to be 'shells' with braces and an internal keel.

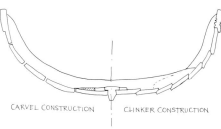

CARVEL CONSTRUCTION | CLINKER CONSTRUCTION

PROPULSION

Sculls – technically these are simply paired oars, but over the past 50 years the term is increasingly used to refer to outrigged racing boats for paired oars. Large barge oars used singly are 'sweeps'.

Randan – *any* boat designed for both rowing and sculling, i.e an oarsman with a single oar at 'bow' and at 'stroke' (nearest the stern), with a sculler with a pair of sculls between them amidships.

BOATS ON THE RIVER

Barges. The older commercial craft of the Thames were floating shallow-draft (depth) flat-bottomed boxes, rather punt-like with sloping ends. They usually had a 'swim-head' bow while the stern was fitted with a vertical fin called a 'budgett' to aid directional stability. 'Swim' heads and 'budgett' sterns may still be seen on present day Thames lighters. Flat-bottomed barges were keel-less, but had a keelson, a bar or bars running the length of the craft to give it longitudinal strength. Barges with a draught of little more than 1 metre

LEEBOARD

SQUARE-RIGGED SWIMHEADED BARGE

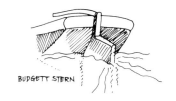

BUDGETT STERN

could carry cargo of 200 tons. But they had to be narrow, usually the beam (width) ratio to length of 1:7. The bottom would be of elm (rot-resistant when wet), the sides of oak. A square sail could be hoisted on a mast placed well forward in an iron 'tabernacle'. A square sail was only raised in the happy event of a following wind. The mast was required as much for towing as for sailing. Square sails were abandoned in the eighteenth century in favour of a spritsail. This consisted of a sprit mainsail, and a foresail mounted forward. A 'mizzen' sail was later added to the stern to assist steering. The addition of the mizzen contributed to the

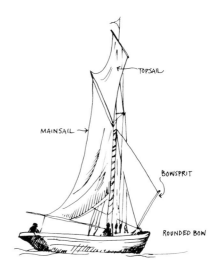

development of the slightly smaller 'stumpie' barge used for up-river work. In the late eighteenth century the average crew for a 140-ton barge consisted of 6 men. 'Leeboards', large paddle shaped pieces of wood, were lowered from the side of the craft into the water on the leeward side to avoid sideways drift when being towed or when sailing to windward, a crucial consideration in a river. Sail-less barges, powered solely by oars or hauling, were known as 'dumb' barges or by the name of the large oars used, 'sweeps'. Sails were normally only used travelling downstream, when use could be made of the prevailing south-westerly wind.

The Thames barge did not reach its final shape, with rounded bow with vertical stem and a transom stern until well into the nineteenth century. First, the swim head gave way to a rounded bow, then to the modern straight stem. A large barge could cover

25 miles daily going upstream and 35 miles travelling down stream. By the 1860s the budgett stern had developed into a deep narrow transom. But there were always basic variations. The estuarine craft were different from those of the Thames and Medway where carrying capacity and shallow draft were more important than speed and stability.

Barges venturing above the tidal flux were 'West Country' barges. They were flat bottomed with straight sides set at right angles to the bottom, with swim-headed bows and a transom stern. They were capable of carrying anything from 25 tons up to 90 tons or so. Many of them brought chalk and peat for use in the market gardens of the lower Thames west of London. Newbury peat ash, containing a high proportion of chalk washed down from the hills, was much used by Middlesex market gardeners. It was dug, dried and burnt reducing it to lime and vegetable ash. Manure was also brought up to the market gardens from London.

Thames barges were able to carry up to 200 tons of cargo but designed to be handled by the smallest possible crew, a skipper and his mate. They could carry enough bricks for a house, and often did. Operating barges tended to be a family activity, with sons taking the place of apprentices or hired hands when they became old enough. The Thames sailing barge reached its peak in the late nineteenth century. In 1879 there were 7,000 barges registered with the Watermen's Company. Almost all the barges on the Thames now are steel and 'Dutch' in design. With the establishment of major waterworks above the tidal Thames, coal was brought up river to provide the energy until electrification became universal in the 1950s.

As one might imagine, there was hot competition for berths at wharves and great pressure to offload quickly. Most river settlements had drawdocks, purpose-built slopes where barge and cart could meet to facilitate offloading. On the tideway offloading was often done on shingle foreshores at low water. A handy skipper would come down the last stretch of river to his destination on the ebb, enjoy low water for offloading and catch the flood to return upriver again. If they could not be sure of a berth against a wharf, those coming in from the estuary would inevitably take twice as long, coming in on the flood, waiting till low water to offload and then awaiting high water in order to return down river. Missing the tide implied a massive loss of time.

Towing: barges were normally hauled on the appropriate ebb or flood tide by gangs of up to 50 men known as 'halers', almost invariably ruffians and convicts, some still in their chains. They struggled with their load along the riverbank where possible, but often waded along the foreshore. Here is an account of boat-halers, given by a Richmond historian in 1866:

> '… all this heavy work which has been now for many years done by horses, was then exclusively done by men, hence the term 'Bargemen'. They were harnessed, if the expression is allowed, seven or eight in number, by means of broad leathern straps, which rested on and around the shoulders of each man; each of these straps being attached to the long rope or tow-line fixed to the barge, they thus hauled the same along the 'Silent Highway'. They worked, as it has been shown, by stages, not very long ones, and thus the loaded vessel by very slow degrees reached its destination. The price paid to the men for this description of work was at per ton, and it has been said that it was very remunerative work to those who were thus employed. [And was doubtless literally a killer.]

> 'They were compelled to live as much together as possible in one particular locality in each place, which would be

naturally near to the river bank; in Richmond the chosen and favourite spot was Water Lane, and when traffic on this side of the river required, as it frequently did in the night, additional or extra assistance, those who sought it would proceed up that neighbourhood with a loud cry or call of 'Man to horse, man to horse'.... [almost certainly a corruption of 'Man to hawse']; but upon hearing the well-known sound, the bargemen would in a few minutes have risen, and be ready to proceed with the vessel and its freight on the opposite shore to the spot appointed for a fresh relay to take it in charge.'

The towropes could be up to 220 yards long. Such was the strain on them that they often had to be replaced after four or so journeys. Just how tough a haler's life was is evident in this short description, written about 1800:

'The rapidity of the current in many places renders this employment a work of great labour, particularly in dry seasons. In passing different weirs, they [the halers] are then obliged to fall with all their force flat on the ground, which is done by the shout of "Yo Ho!" in which position they continue for a short space, when, on another shout being given, they rise up and, securing their step, fall down a second time, and so on till they gain a more peaceful and greater depth of water.'

Horse-towing was introduced in the eighteenth century but only became widespread during the nineteenth. Teams of twelve horses were normally used. The river flow could make a difference of 10mph. Bridges and weirs were a particular problem, particularly going upstream, when extra help was required to pull through a stronger current. The towrope for men and horses was fixed to the mast amidships, which helped to keep the barge away from the bank. It was for horses that towpaths were created, paygates erected and tolls levied by riparian landowners for the upkeep of the tow-path and, of course, for profit. In 1776 the Corporation of the City of London started the compulsory purchase of all the towpath tollgates below Staines, replacing the system of tolls with navigation dues on barges based upon distance and tonnage load, compensating riparian owners on the old basis of the number of two-horses passing the private paygates.

One of the frustrations of barge towing was that either because of private ownership of the bank or because the terrain became unsuitable, halers and horses had periodically to cross from one bank to the other, and this affected the location of ferries. Here is a description of haling upstream from Putney to Kingston:

> 'Up to this period [1774], the towing path on the Surrey side, for the use of barges and vessels conveying heavy goods and merchandise up the river, ended exactly opposite to the first or Railshead Isleworth ferry; here the men who had towed the "craft", as it is termed, from Barnes or Putney were taken off, and returned to the place they had started from, while others on the opposite bank drew loaded barges up as far as "Ragman's Castle" near the well known Ait [Eel Pie Island] at Twickenham: here the towing path again commenced on the Surrey side, and continued as far as Kingston Bridge, where it once more transferred to the Middlesex bank.'

FERRIES

Ferries operated both along the length of and across the river. Originally there were fords, but these disappeared as a result of the rising river level, the creation of weirs, mainly for fishing, and London Bridge which acted like a dam backing the water up the Thames.

Wherries The wherry (no resemblance to cargo-carrying vessels of the same name on the Norfolk Broads) is a rowing boat used to ferry people up and down river. Before rail and road services brought about a collapse of the old system, a ferry service was provided from recognised steps and jetties certainly as far upstream as Hampton, and was manned by licensed watermen (see below). It was normally licensed to carry six or eight persons. It would always travel each way on the tide, thus circumscribing the time and direction of travel. From Richmond, for example a waterman would take three hours on the tide to reach the City of London, and only two if the passenger paid double for a second oarsman, often the waterman's apprentice. On his own the waterman would use a pair of sculls. With his apprentice they would take a single oar each. Larger wherries had a 'randan' rig, for both a pair of oars and a pair of sculls, or even three pairs of sculls.

WHERRY

The wherry is a long rudderless clinker-built craft, with little freeboard (between the surface of the water and the top of the boat's side) and a pointed vertical stern. There are two reasons for this design. A pointed stern does not catch the wind as does a transom stern, an important consideration for the oarsman. It is also less likely to be damaged by other boats coming in to moor at the same crowded steps. By 1700 there were over 100 stairs or landing places within the London area. Most wherry construction took place on the riverbanks of Southwark and Lambeth. Boat builders have constructed wherries to the same design since Viking days. The reason is simple: the Vikings mastered small boat technology and hydrodynamics to perfection. The wherry still closely follows the Viking long-boat in both shape and technology over a thousand years later.

Rowbarges and Shallops   Rowbarges and shallops were the prestigious ferries of the river. Rowbarges could carry up to 100 persons and usually required 20 oarsmen. Almost without exception they were in the

SHALLOP

possession of the Corporation of the City of London or the London livery companies. They were the visual demonstration of their financial power. The shallop was the 'Daimler' of the river, built for royalty and the nobility, powered by six oars.

Skiffs   Until the mid-nineteenth century skiffs were clinker-built boats for crossing the river. They were shorter, narrower and

DOUBLE SKIFF

slower than the wherry. The narrowness was necessary because they were side loading and, if wider, would tip easily while passengers were boarding or alighting (The wherry was bow-loading, because of boats crowding around the ferry steps.)

Flats were ferries for livestock and carts.

Steam craft In 1813 the first steam craft, *Richmond*, plied for hire between Richmond and London. It was unsuccessful and a second *Richmond*, 62 ft long and copper bottomed, plied for hire from 1815 until its boiler burst two years later. From 1840 the *Locomotive* provided the first regular service between Hampton Court and London. Steam craft found operating on the upper tidal Thames extremely difficult after demolition of old London Bridge until the creation of the Richmond half-lock in 1898.

Peterboats, or fishing boats Named after the patron saint of fisher-men, these were used as net fishing boats. A peterboat was double ended and of clinker construction with a wide beam, a 'wet well' within the boat and a 'catchbox' floating astern just below the surface (making towing significantly easier on its way to market at Billingsgate). Under sail it carried a simple spritsail and foresail. The last peterboat net licence was issued in the 1930s to the Gibson family, Strand on the Green.

Narrow boats Narrow (or 'monkey') boats, built as canal freighters, became a common sight on the Thames with the completion of the Oxford and Grand Union canals in the 1790s and now remain as a popular leisure craft. Originally they were horse-drawn. Their rounded bows, an attempt to minimise damage to the clay lining of canal beds, influenced barge design in the nineteenth century.

WATERMEN

Until the beginning of the sixteenth century, getting a boat up, down or across the river was a matter of bargaining and a source of major irritation for travellers. In 1514 Henry VIII established the Company of Watermen of the Thames. It was not like the livery companies which existed to protect the interests of their membership, but was established to protect the interests of the travelling public against rapacious watermen. Only registered watermen could ply their trade and a table of standard fares was drawn up. In Pepys' time there were some 10,000 licensed watermen. They were all required to wear the badge of Watermans' Hall or that of their employer to prove they had served their seven-year apprenticeship.

The press gang was a major problem for watermen. Barge-masters and their mates often commissioned elderly crew at Kingston for the final leg of the journey to London, so as to avoid the acute danger of their being press-ganged into the navy. Apprentices were also exempt from empressment, and they were careful to carry their papers downstream of Kingston. Watermen who joined the local fire brigade or were employed by a peer of the realm were also immune from the press gang. By the nineteenth century ordinary watermen wore short blue jackets, while the sovereign's watermen wore scarlet.

PLEASURE BOATS

Boating for pleasure was a reprieve for Thames watermen in Richmond after the advent of rail and horse-drawn omnibuses, which had destroyed the wherry business. The middle classes, arriving by train from the 1850s onward, wished to play on the river and watermen were never so busy. In response to the demand, Mr Messum of Richmond devised a 'pleasure skiff', essentially an evolution of the wherry but with a narrow transom stern. By the mid-1930s about 4,000 pleasure craft were licensed with the Port of London Authority for the stretch between Richmond and Teddington locks. Indeed, commercial pleasure craft were not allowed to operate on the fully tidal Thames below Richmond except on specific occasions. During the inter-war years there were 26 boating firms operating between Glover's Island, opposite

Petersham, and the railway bridge downstream, but of these six were large ones each with approximately 100 boats. These six were essentially family businesses: Redknap, Chitty (see vol. 1, p. 208), Peasley, Wheeler, Messum and Light. Trade was fairly shared. Each business could only ply for trade on a short stretch of the river. There were four plying grounds, (i) from the pier above Richmond Bridge down to the boathouses just below the bridge; (ii) from the boathouses to the waterfront below the War Memorial (just before the *Slug & Lettuce*); (iii) from the waterfront below the War Memorial to Water Lane; (iv) from the *White Cross Hotel* to Friars Lane.

At the beginning of business each day a board would be set up at each plying ground, with slots for each firm's card. The top card had an option on the first job of the day: one hour for one shilling, or five shillings for boat hire all day. Once the top card firm had hired out a boat, its card went to the bottom, just like a taxi rank. However, unlike a taxi rank, the top firm might decline a hire if the request was for only an hour on a fine day, in favour of getting first option for an all day hiring at 5/-. The option for the hour's outing would pass down the list until a firm was happy to take the business. The further down the daily board the firm was, the more willing it was to hire out for a shorter time and lower fee, simply because one had less far to drop to the bottom of the list. On a dull day more money might be made by taking whatever came up, rather than holding out for an all-day hiring. It was all a question of judgment. Dog racing, introduced in 1921, sounded the first death knell of boating. Young gentlemen preferred to take their ladies to the dogs, and boating continued steadily downhill as other attractions also drew people away from the river. Eel Pie island was a favoured boating destination, while Corporation Island, opposite the Richmond Bridge boathouses, was favoured for nocturnal assignations.

Yet before the Second World War there were plenty of people in Richmond itself who frequently went out boating. The large department stores like Goslings and Wrights in George Street had dormitories at the top of the shop for their young assistants. These young men would go boating in the summer after the day's work. They simply took the boats out, brought them back, sometimes after midnight and settled up with the hirer later. It was considered bad form for the hirer to ask for payment or a deposit beforehand.

Stan Peasley, descended from watermen who had run the ferry before the building of Richmond Bridge, was first apprenticed in 1937. His apprenticeship took seven years but it got him off formal school as it was considered an education. He had already started to earn as a young lad. He used to hang around Richmond Station and offer to carry hampers, cushions and gramophones down to the river. He could earn more by offering to carry this paraphernalia back to the station at the end of the day.

By the 1960s Peasley had expanded into motor boats, up to 60 of them. For every boat hired out he maintained a spare engine in case of breakdown. He prided himself on being able to replace the engine of a boat in 4 minutes. The business, like ice cream vending, was hugely contingent on the weather. Ironically however, the heat wave year of 1976 was the worst year ever. The drought drained the river, which began to stink with piles of rubbish and stagnant water. Boats that were taken out frequently ran aground in the rubbish.

Today there are two firms left: Mark Edwards who both builds and hires out rowing boats, and Mike Turk of Kingston who runs the river launches that ply between Richmond and Hampton Court.

APPENDIX 2

Race-rowing and the Boat Race

The first formalised race on record was between watermen using sculls. In 1716 Mr Thomas Doggett, a comedy actor, donated money for a new coat and badge to be annually competed for by six newly qualified watermen on 1 August, the date of George 1's accession. The competitors were to row from London Bridge to Chelsea. Why? Partly because Doggett loved rowing but also because he was 'a Whig up to the head and ears', loved the Hanoverian monarchy and wished to commemorate its defeat of the 1715 Jacobite Rising. The coat was originally Orange (now red), the colour of Protestant ascendancy, and the badge depicted the White Horse of the House of Hanover.

This was the beginning of race-rowing on the Thames. As with racing eights, technical improvements (see below) transformed the sport and inevitably led to a parting of the ways between watermen plying their trade and racing, which henceforth took place in custom-built sculling boats. A leading light in the process was Frederick Furnivall (see p.173), but see also Tom Green's story, p.117.

Competitive team rowing between students began about 200 years ago. Oxford undergraduates were rowing to Iffley and Nuneham by the 1790s. A Mrs Hooper hired out rowing clothes: long trousers, jacket and a catskin cap. In 1815 Oxford students apparently rowed their first eight-oared races in stovepipe hats. A decade later an Oxford crew rowed to London in a single day, a distance of 140 miles. Even with the flow of the tide this was a formidable achievement in a heavy cutter with fixed seats and no outriggers. They had to row part of the tideway against the flood. Members of the crew had to be carried ashore on arrival in the City.

The 1829 Oxford boat set alongside a racing eight of 1923, half the beam but longer and with fixed pin outriggers. The 1829 boat, with oars, weighed 441kg. By the 1920s a racing eight, with oars, weighed 160kg. Today's boats weigh only 96kg, with oars a total of about 115kg.

In February 1829 Cambridge challenged Oxford to race, the course being from Hambledon Lock to Henley Bridge, Oxford in blue-check vests and black straw hats, Cambridge in white with a pink necktie worn as a waistband. Oxford won. The average weight seems to have been little over 11 stones. Today the average weight is three stones heavier. But today's crews are lightweight in other respects. Between them, the 1829 boats produced two bishops, George Selwyn, first bishop of New Zealand, and Charles Words-worth, bishop of St Andrews, as well as three eminent deans, of Ripon, Lincoln and Ely. All of them wrote learned works.

Exhausted by that experience, the next race was not until 1836, from Westminster Bridge to Putney Bridge. From 1856 it became an annual event. In 1852 the Leander boat, shadowing the two blue boats, sank bow first. The cox, who could not swim, said to stroke

(the stern oarsman) 'Give me your oar, Sir, for I cannot swim.'
'Neither can I, sir,' replied the stroke, gallantly handing him his oar.
Those were the days.

TECHNICAL ADVANCES

The first races were made in clinker-built (see p.225) cutters made
of oak. They were extremely heavy, consisting of nine strakes, or
planks, between keel and gunwale. During the nineteenth century
there was a succession of technical innovations that transformed
the speed of the boats. In 1841 Oxford used a carvel boat, smooth
skinned but with a keel. In 1846 the first public trial with outriggers
was made. They folded into the boat when not in use. Metal outriggers were the brainchild of a Tyneside boat-builder, Harry
Clasper, who had come south. He realised that an outrigger, putting
the pivotal point of the oar beyond the gunwale, greatly increased
the leverage of the oarsman, and therefore the power of the stroke. It
must have been shortly thereafter that a wager-, or racing-, boat for
sculls was built along Furnivall's (see p.173) new slim lines, for the
champion sculler, Newell. Newell challenged Clasper to a race
knowing Clasper was very seldom beaten. On this occasion Clasper
was outclassed but one cannot help thinking he must have been
delighted to find himself vanquished using his own technology.

In 1857 Oxford used a carvel keel-less boat made by another
Tyneside boat-builder, Matthew Taylor. In fact the keel was laid
inside the boat. This 'Newcastle boat' was less stable but much
faster in the water. Good balance by the crew now became a
fundamental requirement to win the race. Oxford won by more than
half a minute. Both crews also used rounded oar blades for the first
time. They could catch the water more effectively. In 1873 both boats
adopted sliding seats, an American innovation. Like outriggers,
they dramatically changed the speed of the boat, since these again

greatly increased the oarsmen's length of stroke in the water. The first time they were used the oarsmen still placed their feet on the bottom of the boat. It was extremely uncomfortable and the problem was solved with 'stretchers', adjustable and angled footplates, giving the sliding seat its greatest potential.

BOAT-BUILDING

Harry Clasper and Matthew Taylor were the two great racing boat builders of the nineteenth century. In the twentieth century their place was taken by George Sims of Putney, then of Eel Pie Island, Twickenham. Whereas his forerunners had improved the technical performance of boats, Sims made very finely finished and significantly lighter craft. Modern timber cutting enabled the production of thin sheeting, so he built craft with a hull of barely half a centimetre in thickness, the shell wrapped onto the internal keel and ribs of the boat. These 'shell' eights became imperative for racing. Sims could work fast if he had to. In 1934 the Oxford coach ordered a new boat. Sims delivered it in 72 working hours, for cash and a barrel of beer. Wooden 'shell' eights were displaced by 'Carbocraft' fibreglass boats in the 1970s. Oars changed shape, first to 'Macon' or 'spade' oars in 1960, then in the 1990s to 'cleaver' oars and were also made of fibreglass.

ROWING AND CLASS

Until very recently rowing was the sport of toffs. At first Eton College and Westminster School were the only two rowing schools, but they were soon imitated by other public schools. It was not long before the snobbery of amateurism made itself felt. In 1839 a Cambridge man publicly proposed 'to allow no waterman to have anything to do with the matches, but to leave it all to gentlemen.'

Watermen still coached both boat crews. They knew what they were doing, for their lives were predicated on rowing the river with speed and economy of effort. In 1846 an Oxford cox made the breathtaking observation: 'A coxswain ought to be a thinking, reasoning being, in a higher degree than any waterman has yet shown himself to be.' The fact is that one simply did not want chaps of the lower orders telling toffs what to do. In their ignorant snobbery, both universities rejected the canniest and most experienced oars on the river.

THE TIDEWAY COURSE

The course is 4¼ miles long, starting about 100 metres upstream of Putney Bridge and ending the same distance short of Chiswick Bridge. Traditionally the Surrey station has been viewed as the more advantageous, on account of the long bend around Barnes. But the initial advantage lies on the Middlesex station and a crew on this side, if it can gain an initial length's lead, may then follow the best of the tide and need only move over if the pursuing crew catches it up.

TACTICS

Clearly the best crew, save for misfortune, will win. Beyond supreme fitness, the oarsmen require several essential individual and collective skills: the most important individual skill is to produce full and powerful strokes, lifting the blade cleanly out of the water at the end of each stroke, turning the blade almost to horizontal once out of the water (to improve the aerodynamics and avoid crabs), returning it to the vertical position before 'catching' the water at the beginning the next stroke. The collective skills are arguably more important, summarised in the words: *balance* and *timing*. If the boat runs smoothly without rocking and the blades all enter and leave the water together, things are good. The final contest-

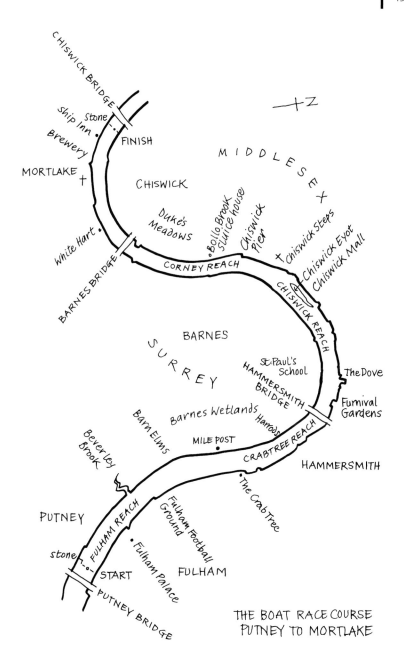

THE BOAT RACE COURSE
PUTNEY TO MORTLAKE

winning ingredient for the oarsmen is the ability rapidly to step up the 'strike rate', and therefore speed, in order to gain leadership in the race and thereby to enjoy the dominating position. But to be able to do this at junctures of one's own choosing, a crew must be not only supremely fit but supremely 'together', something that goes beyond the physical into the boat's collective state of mind. As all oarsmen know, as a race drains every last ounce of strength the desire to die becomes acute. Under such circumstances of extreme exhaustion maintaining that state of togetherness becomes immensely difficult, mentally much more than physically, particularly if the adversary is ahead. The losing crew faces a far more Herculean struggle. Theirs is the real triumph over adversity.

The other vital skill belongs to the cox: an acute feeling for the ways of the river. Since the river is tidal, and the race commences near the top of the flood tide, it is to the advantage of the boat to enjoy the centre of that tidal flow. The great puzzle, however, is where is that centre? The course is like a large s-bend, so the tidal flow is anything but straight. The other problem is that the Thames is notoriously windy and the direction of the wind varies with every bend. Virtually every occasion when a boat has sunk has been because of wind.

If one boat gets ahead it is allowed to take the other boat's water, but must give way if the other boat catches up. The real danger lies in the period before one crew has achieved the dominant position. Both coxes tend to steer towards the other, to contest the middle water. Even if they do not clash it can still be bad for boat speed, since they must steer out again to avoid collision. Aerial photography shows that boats neck and neck seldom row parallel: they converge only to diverge, but then repeat the process while the umpire tries to avoid their clashing. The task of the cox is lonely, nerve-racking and anything but easy.

APPENDIX 3

Landscape, buildings and suburbia near the Thames

BRICKS

Most of us know little about the basic building block that almost all our homes are made of. Building in brick had occurred sporadically but increasingly in eastern and south-eastern England through the later Middle Ages, usually in response to the lack of readily available stone. For large structures of the magnate class, its real disadvantage was that it could not withstand assault as readily as stone. By the mid-fifteenth century, brick started to be much more widely used. Henry VI used it at Richmond Palace and the Brigittines at Syon. In the Tudor period, brick arrived as a thoroughly fashionable material. It had real advantages: it could be manufactured on site; it came in standard shapes not needing to be cut or dressed; and it was easy to use, sized literally to be handy. Finally, it was elastic. Large expanses of brick and lime mortar had tensile strength to endure expansion and contraction or even endure considerable settlement, as can be seen on any number of pre-1900 house facades in London.

At first the master brick builders were Dutch or Flemish and brick was expensively imported. By 1500, however, brick was made as close to the building site as possible. In 1502, for example, Brentford manufactured 400,000 bricks for Syon Abbey. The raw material, 'brick earth' or sandy clay, was readily available or mixable in most river valleys, including the Thames. By the late Middle Ages there was an accepted seasonal calendar: the brick earth was to be dug out before winter set in. It was left in heaps to be 'cured' or broken down by frost and rain. In spring it was 'puddled' (pulverised) into dough and worked over with shovels, the stones and other foreign bodies removed. Chalk would be broken up and mixed in to reduce the tendency of bricks to crack during drying or explode when firing. Bricks were moulded and left 'green' in loose 'hackstacks' to dry out thoroughly, usually for not less than eight weeks. Finally, they would be stacked in a kiln or in 'clamps', with layers of cinder between the courses. Flues would be left open and filled with brushwood. Once the clamp was well alight the flues would be closed and the clamp allowed to burn itself out over the next two to four weeks. The colour of the brick was affected by the material and temperature at which it was fired. The smell was terrible. Brown bricks are characteristic of the Thames valley. London yellow 'stocks' were much preferred to red through most of the eighteenth and nineteenth centuries. Brick manufacture and building reached its climax in England in the mid-nineteenth century when the industrial revolution and railways led to an unprecedented explosion of many towns and cities.

There are several methods of bricklaying but two to look out for on these walks. The humble and handy brick exposes one surface to the world: its length, the 'stretcher', or its end, the 'header'. Flemish bond, in which headers and stretchers alternate in a single course, has become the virtually universal bond used in Britain. Early brickwork, however, is normally in 'English' bond. It alternated courses of headers and courses of stretchers, but went progressively out of fashion

ENGLISH BOND

FLEMISH BOND

in the late seventeenth century, to be replaced almost entirely with Flemish bond. If one cannot tell age by building style, the brick bond will indicate whether the structure you are looking at is likely to be pre- or post-1700. But one should bear in mind that there is any amount of repair work done to pre-1700 structures using Flemish bond or imitative English bond. Patched areas are often a bodge between these two bonds.

DEVELOPMENT TO THE ENGLISH LANDSCAPE GARDEN AND PALLADIAN ARCHITECTURE

The idea of the 'pleasure' Thames reached its cultural climax in the first three decades of the eighteenth century with the development of the landscape garden, which largely took place close to the Thames between Hampton and Chiswick, notably at Richmond Gardens and Kew Gardens (Walk 3), and Chiswick House (Walk 5).

During the Middle Ages and the Tudor period a garden tended to be enclosed as a courtyard surrounded by buildings or attached to a building's side (see vol. I, p. 255). In the seventeenth century a quiet revolution began. Francis Bacon's essay 'Of Gardens' (1597), though a personal view, offered fresh thinking. Bacon wanted something quite different from gardens of the past. He proposed a garden set out in three visual parts: 'a green in the entrance [from the house], a heath or desert in the going forth; and the main garden in the midst.' The heath he calls 'a natural wilder-ness. Trees I would have none in it, but some thickets, made only of sweet briar and honeysuckle, and some wild vine amongst' but for the side grounds, 'you are to fill them with a variety of alleys, private, to give full shade, some of them, wheresoever the sun be.' No tans then, since he favoured 'a covert alley, upon carpenter's work, about twelve foot in height….' Perhaps the most striking requirement however, is an unimpeded view 'for letting your prospect from the hedge, through the arches, upon the heath.' Gardens may have remained largely formal but suddenly one can discern two crucial new features for the seventeenth century garden: a relationship with the house and a vista that leads the eye into the middle distance.

During the next fifty years the wilderness developed as a geometric pattern of alleys letting onto open areas in which other features might be found. A tall fir tree was often favoured at the centre. Each alley was intended to give a view, possibly with a statue or urn, or building as the focal point. Until 1700 gardens remained highly formalised geometric gardens with statuary, fountains, clipped hedges, elaborated patterned gravel and turf *parterres*, open areas of low growing plants, laid out in scroll patterns or 'broderie', a successor to knots, of which Bacon would probably not have approved either, and avenues of trees forming narrow vistas.

If there was one overriding characteristic with the prevailing style of gardening at the very beginning of the eighteenth century one might say it was still the idea of Man in dominion over Nature. This type of gardening reached its ultimate form in the work of the great French gardener, Le Nôtre, who laid out Versailles. English garden style was heavily affected by this formalism, as well as a fondness for statuary and topiary. Such gardens articulated the power and authority of the owner.

The revolution in British gardening came through a confluence of sympathetic influences. Most importantly, a number of influential Britons made the Grand Tour to Italy, taking Horace and Virgil as their literary companions, both of whom extolled the virtues of rural life. In Italy they saw the paintings of Claude and Poussin who painted the Roman Campagna as an idealised and harmonious landscape replete with relics of antiquity. Such travellers were stimulated to look at nature and also classical architecture afresh.

It was not long before a political connection was made, the 'formal mockery of princely gardens' being identified with French absolute monarchy, and the growing British interest in 'Nature' being associated with the idea of Liberty. In reality, of course, the idea of 'Nature' was a highly contrived and controlled version of the natural landscape, but it suggested a harmony between individual liberty and the rule of law. Mindful of the words of the political philosopher, John Locke, 'Where there is no law there is no freedom,' this was a theme with which the British gentry of the eighteenth century were particularly pre-occupied.

Similar observations might be made about the development of British country house architecture. Responsibility for the enormous visual change lay initially with a small coterie of literary and artistic luminaries. Some of them became intimately involved with the developments along the Thames: Alexander Pope, William Kent (see below), Lord Burlington, Henry Herbert (later 9th Earl of Pembroke), James Gibbs (see below), Colen Campbell (see below), and later Lancelot 'Capability' Brown. With the exceptions of Pope and Brown, all these had made the Grand Tour and returned imbued with ideas of classical landscape and architecture. With the exception of Gibbs, their architectural interest had been attracted by the work of the sixteenth century Italian, Andrea Palladio, who had studied the writings of the great Roman architectural theorist of the first century BC, Vitruvius. Palladio, and his early English disciple, Inigo Jones, put them in touch with classical architecture that reinforced their belief in Man in harmony with Nature. Palladio offered them, through the many villas he designed for Venetian landowners, examples of classical architecture adapted to the requirements of the country gentleman. Palladio's architectural principles, particularly proportion and symmetry, seemed the material and harmonious embodiment of Locke's ideas of liberty and order. There might, in the words of one English gentleman, be an apparent 'state of contrariety' between buildings and landscape, but 'as fabrics should be regular, so gardens should be irregular.' Palladian architecture set in an idealised natural landscape came to be seen as the visual embodiment of Whig Constitutionalism.

SOME RELEVANT ARCHITECTS

James Gibbs (1682-1754) is, in the words of John Summerson, 'best described as the delayed fulfilment of Wren.' Gibbs was the only professionally trained architect in Britain of his day. The Palladians, for example Burlington, Campbell, Kent, were all comparative amateurs. Gibbs had studied architecture in Rome under the tutelage of one of the great teachers of the baroque, Carlo Fontana. It was partly as a result of this training and his own self-assurance that Gibbs always remained apart from the Palladian movement. But Gibbs (properly Gibb) was also a Scot, a Tory and a Catholic, a combination that immediately raised the Jacobite question in Whig minds. Furthermore, Gibbs had trained for the priesthood in Rome before deciding on a career in architecture. So his political and religious sympathies made him suspect, particularly after his first work, St Mary-le-Strand (1714), exhibited such dangerously Italian baroque features. It was a little akin to building a Soviet-style building in Washington at the height of the Cold War, a real provocation. In the face of adverse comment Gibbs restrained his subsequent work until the very end of his career, when his passion for the Italian baroque is apparent in the Radcliffe Camera, Oxford (1739).

Colen Campbell (1676-1729). Campbell's significance lies in his revival of the architectural style of Palladio in and around London, after its initial introduction by Inigo Jones a century earlier. Like Gibbs, Campbell was a Scot, the son of a laird in Nairnshire. He was a star law pupil in Edinburgh, but he acquired an interest in architecture, studied it, and following the Acts of Union in 1707, established himself as an architect in England. His first commission was Wanstead House in Essex, no longer standing. He was invited to put *Vitruvius Britannicus* together by a small group of patrons with the money for such an ambitious scheme. His first volume 'decisively shaped the development of classical architecture in eighteenth century England'. In the words of Dr Tim Connor, 'the text of his introduction was a powerful statement of pride in the achievement of British architects, a call to order against the extravagance of Italian baroque for which the example of Palladio, mediated by Inigo Jones was the ideal corrective.' Campbell was eclipsed by Burlington himself, a more skilful and inventive student of Palladio.

William Kent (1686-1748) was an artist, architect and landscaper, but it was thanks to the last skill that he really made his name, at Chiswick House and the White House in Kew Gardens among other places (Walk 5). He made a greater contribution to the development of the Palladian garden style than any of his contemporaries.

Kent came from more humble origins than either Gibbs or Campbell, his father being a Yorkshire joiner. Arriving in London he had a series of lucky breaks, meeting many of the London *glitterati*, notably Pope, Handel and Gay. He met Burlington while studying in Rome. His impulsive character charmed the austere Burlington, initiating a life-long friendship and the collaboration of opposites. Walpole was a great admirer of his work, crediting him as the one who 'invented the new style', who had 'leaped the fence and discovered that all nature was a garden' and who was 'the inventor of an art that realises painting and improves Nature'. Kent worked at Twickenham (the results sadly now all gone save the grotto), at Stowe, Bucks, and Rousham, Oxon, where his work may still be admired. Closer to home, he remodelled Bridgeman's garden at Esher, now Claremont, a National Trust Property. He had been asked to extend Bridgeman's work there and render the whole more informal, and it is there that you can see Kent arguably at his best, in Horace Walpole's words, 'Kent is Kentissime there.'

THE SUBURBAN VILLA

On almost every walk, one encounters some suburban housing and it may be helpful to place it in some sort of context. The eighteenth century had marked the arrival of the leisured and rural gentry class. The nineteenth century marked the arrival of the professional middle classes and those of lower status to service them and this, along with their technical innovations, changed the character of the Thames in a way in which the arrival of the gentry had not done. The Thames was progressively transformed from a transport facility into a leisure facility. The development of railway in the middle years brought about the wholesale suburbanisation of the Thames valley up to Hampton and with it, the despoliation of this stretch of the Thames.

Much of the time we dismiss suburban housing without so much as a glance. But it is hoped that this brief introduction will sharpen your appreciation of where we live, even if it does mar Elysium.

A few observations may make trudging down suburban streets more rewarding. Why, compared with other European cities, did England largely eschew flats? In part it was because England was so orderly. It experienced nothing of the street mobs that raged through European capitals in 1848 nor the memory of besieging armies which demanded tightly drawn defences. English towns and cities could be open and vulnerable, almost 'garden' cities. Furthermore, personal status was visible and apparent in one's dwelling. Flats were associated with tenements, tenements with welfare and welfare with poverty. The middle classes and below them the artisan and labouring classes all wished to emulate their social superiors with dwellings standing in gardens that indicated substance, owner-ship and most of all, personal freedom and independence, a very English trait. Social pretensions were reflected in the facades of the houses. Even labourers' cottages suggested rural lifestyle, itself deemed superior to urban tenement existence. The English have always imagined they are reluctant city-dwellers and many certainly like to grow food in their back gardens, a fantasy of rural self-sufficiency. Pretensions were also reflected in the abandonment of the term 'street', associated with the overcrowded and impoverished inner city, in favour of 'road', with its more rural association. By the end of the century suburbia was replete with other superior terms: 'grove', 'park' and 'avenue', all suggesting a faintly gentrified form of rural life. With the Arts and Crafts Movement at the end of the century street terms of disingenuous rusticity were adopted: 'way' and 'close'. But by then almost all the Thames between Richmond and Putney had been developed.

After 1918 almost all the remaining Thames valley market gardens disappeared and another phase of building occurred. In almost every suburb down the Thames it is possible to notice pre-suburbia at the heart of an old village, and then zones of Victorian, Edwardian, between the two wars, and post-War suburban housing. The other characteristic is 'in-filling' when a large Victorian villa, for example, was demolished to make room for several smaller dwellings, or the garden assigned for more dwellings. Walk 1, through East Twickenham, gives examples of the infilling of pasture and park during the past century. These kinds of development can be noted as one walks down streets of varying vintage.

Georgian or even pre-Georgian houses will be found at the heart of virtually every town or village centre between Hampton and Fulham. Early Victorians favoured the 'Italianate' style but this gave way to 'Gothic' (a term which rapidly meant anything other than classical). Why did the Victorians abandon Georgian architecture, with its unrivalled elegance and felicitous proportion? Perhaps the most immediate reason was that Georgian terraces sported generally unrelieved facades and symmetry for the whole, and so denied individuality. The new aspiring middle class wanted to stress individual status and this could be done more easily through asymmetric detached and semi-detached Gothic, with assertive front bays and gables, with fancy decorative work over the windows, doors and even on the roof. Perhaps the Gothic Revival was also identified with churches and suggested respectability in an age when the middle classes were expected to attend church.

In the last years of the nineteenth century the Gothic Revival began to be challenged by the Vernacular Movement, which extolled the domesticity of pre-Georgian town houses and country cottages. Its best examples are the 'Arts & Crafts' houses designed by people like Voysey and Lutyens, suggestive of a late medieval or Tudor English countryside, but one must look further afield for these. 'Queen Anne Revival', an amalgam of different vernacular styles drawn mainly from Kent and Sussex but precious little to do with Queen Anne, was developed largely by Norman Shaw. Its characteristics were red brick with white stone facings, dormer windows, massive chimneys, and huge red tiled roofs. Queen Anne Revival soon found itself in competition with other styles based upon an eclectic borrowing of local cottage characteristics: half timbering from Herefordshire and Cheshire, harled exteriors (now known as pebbledash) from the North and Scotland, timber weather boards, herringbone brickwork and tiles from Sussex. It was from this fertile mix that a Vernacular style emerged, its most familiar examplars now known as mock-Tudor and 'Jacobethan'.

Meanwhile the bungalow had arrived from India, at first appealing to the upper middle class as a seaside retreat. Bungalows soon got everywhere, including the more rural stretches of the Thames where again, bungalows (and houseboats) suggested a leisured Thirties lifestyle in which people played golf or bowls by day and sipped G&Ts as they played bridge by night. These dwellings so strongly suggest an era and life style it is difficult not to fantasise about what goes on in them.

Until the 1950s most houses were built in the Vernacular Style. In the first half of the 1930s '*Moderne*' homes, inspired by the functional fundamentalism of Walter Gropius, enjoyed a brief vogue. With their flat roofs and metal-framed windows often with curved glass panes, they are worth looking out for (Walk 1). They had been largely abandoned by 1938. English taste was too conservative. Local authorities usually used neo-Georgian for public buildings and it was only after they abandoned it in favour of 'functional' architecture in the 1950s that neo-Georgian facades became acceptable to the private sector and then became fashionably identified with the upwardly mobile during the Thatcher decade (Walk 6, Corney Reach).

APPENDIX 4

Trees and mycorrhizal fungi

Even discounting Kew Gardens, one finds oneself looking at many trees along the riverbank. Like me, you possibly need an explanation of these miraculous giants.

ROOTS AND SHOOTS

If you were asleep during biology class at school, as I was, you may also need a brief explanation of how trees work. An exchange occurs between the two extremities of a tree, the roots and the shoots. The roots acquire water and nutrients from the soil. The shoot (trunk, branches and leaves) makes sugar, which it pumps to the root.

Looking at the process a little more closely, the root pumps nutrients into the inner cell cavity, or vacuole, using the energy derived from sugar. With this energy it pumps nutrients to the shoot.

TREE TRANSPORT SYSTEM

As you will probably have guessed, one system of tubes pumps water and nutrients from the root to the shoot, the other brings back sugar from the shoot to the root. Water is the transport system for nutrients. The 'tubes', or vessels, are composed of cells joined end to end, which drip-feed each other. In drought the system has much greater difficulty pumping nutrients to the shoots and will ultimately fail.

The trunk is composed of old transport routes, discarded at the end of each season. In other words, it is principally a skeleton, with the 'live' transport routes being those just under the bark. Each year's growth forms layers of cells. The inner ring is known as *xylem*. An outer layer, known as *phloem*, carries energy as starch or sugar down to the root system. The trunk stores nutrients to enable a tree to survive the winter and also to provide the reserve of energy to kick-start the growth of shoots in the spring. Remove a ring of bark and the *phloem* will fail to function. The consequence is that the tree will seem alright for a while, as the water and nutrients continue to be conveyed to the shoot system. But the return of starch to the roots and nutrient storage system will have collapsed, and after a while the tree will die. After each season, the old vessels remain active, as 'sapwood', but their performance progressively slows down. Once no longer functional, these dead cells slowly fill with a durable hard substance (*lignin*) and become 'heartwood', the core of the tree that gives it its strength. The process takes about 20 years.

OSMOSIS

Tree vessels transport their moisture through the process of osmosis: one cell will abstract moisture from a neighbouring cell until both are equally moist. Osmosis does not, however, explain how a tree can raise moisture to a height of 50 metres or more. If you draw water up a tube by a pump, the column of water will break after a height of nine metres, creating a vacuum. In theory, then, a tree should not be able to grow beyond this height. The conducting tubes of a tree are sufficiently narrow that capillary action assists the process. Here is the amazing bit. Even the foregoing is insufficient to explain a column of water being drawn to a height of 100 metres in the case, for example, of 26 Californian redwoods. Every time we stand in front of a tall tree, we stand before a miracle, ancient and modern.

THE LEAF

One can see the veins on most deciduous leaves, the basic transport system for water and nutrients. Given insufficient water, with either a failure of supply from the roots or evaporation in excessive heat, and the system will begin to break down. Leaf type affects how the system works. During the daytime deciduous leaves open pores to release excess moisture and to absorb carbon dioxide. These pores close at night to prevent water loss. Conifers have waxy needles which reduce moisture loss, thus being better able to endure extremes of climate. Most conifers can hibernate without dropping their leaves and are able to put on a growth spurt in the spring. Deciduous trees have leaves with only a very thin waxy layer, which cannot halt evaporation. Their mechanism to prevent water loss over winter is to drop their leaves. Deciduous trees tend to grow in environments with a greater availability of nutrients and water, like along the riverbank. Conifers, by contrast, can endure relatively poor soils and stressful environments. Any conifers you spot along the Thames riverbank have been deliberately planted. Unlike deciduous trees, they are unable to give much useful waste back to the soil.

MYCORRHIZAL FUNGI

Mycorrhizal fungi, the networks of underground fungal filaments, live in symbiosis with tree roots. A fungal system can spread for hundreds of metres underground. Some can also live for as much as 400 years. The filaments are called *hypha* (pl. *hyphae*). Mycorrhizal fungi are very efficient at acquiring nutrients, but have greater difficulty acquiring sugar for energy. A gift exchange takes place: the tree roots supply sugar to the fungus, while the fungus offers nutrients, notably phosphorous.

This, you might be thinking, demonstrates a gratifyingly co-operative spirit. It is much more than that. It is now believed that without the occurrence of mycorrhizal fungi, plants might never have become terrestrial. They would have remained marine plants only.

We are speaking Silurian times here, over 400 million years ago. It is reckoned that over 80 per cent of land plants form these symbiotic relationships.

Mycorrhizal fungi affect which trees may survive in a given area since many such fungi are host-specific, allowing one species to flourish while making it hard for an invading species to establish itself. Think of the colourful and deadly looking fly agaric, the red-headed toadstool with white spots. It flourishes in coniferous areas. Deciduous woodland mycorrhizal fungi are less host-specific. As you walk, remember the intricate network underground that helps make these trees happen.

APPENDIX 5

Brewing beer in London

BEER PRODUCTION

Beer production requires a series of processes to convert grain starch
to sugar, to extract the sugar with water, then to sterilise it by
boiling, cooling and fermentation with yeast in order to produce
an alcoholic drink. The technical words, significantly, are all
Germanic in origin.

- 'Malting' is the first essential step. Barley is soaked, or
  'steeped', in water, then thrown onto the floor and turned over at
  an even temperature to allow germination. It is then dried in a
  kiln. The malt house may be adjacent to the brewery, but could
  as easily be close to barley fields.
- The dried malt is milled to break the starch into particles but
  retain the husk.
- The result, 'grist', is mixed with warm water, becoming 'mash',
  and the conversion of starch into fermentable sugars is then
  completed.
- The liquid, or 'wort', is strained off.
- Hops (dried in a kiln, or oasthouse, after picking) are added
  and the wort is boiled to extract the hop flavours, to arrest
  enzyme activity and sterilise it. It is this boiling which creates
  the characteristic smell associated with breweries.
- Cooled and oxygenated wort is fermented with added yeast,
  and then matured, in a slow or secondary fermentation, which
  produces carbon dioxide, both carbonating the drink but also
  removing volatile compounds
- Traditional or 'real' ale continues to be casked in oak and
  whole hops added.

A THUMBNAIL HISTORY OF LONDON'S
ALES AND BEERS

'A man is never happy for the present' according to Samuel Johnson, 'but when he is drunk.' London agreed with him: in 1618 there were 400 taverns in the City alone. By 1871, London boasted 20,000 pubs and beer shops.

Ale has been made for over 8,000 years, the earliest known records being from Sumer in Mesopotamia. Barley has long been the preferred feedstock but other sources of starch, wheat or oats can also be used. In the Middle Ages ale was made by top fermentation: yeast rising to the surface of the fermentation and skimmed off, which still remains the usual method of production in Britain. In the early fifteenth century Germany developed a new process of cool fermentation in winter, where the yeast settled to the bottom. The ale was stored, cooled by ice, during the summer months and became known as lager (German *lagern*: to store).

Ale got into the lifeblood of London early. By the late twelfth century there were a number of breweries along the river. Traces of London's beery history still lie along the riverbank and Londoners continue to out-drink the rest of the nation. If you wonder why breweries are sited close to the river, for every pint of water going into the beer up to ten pints may be used for washing equipment, casks, or for steaming or cooling.

Brewing was a cottage industry throughout the Middle Ages, often engaged in by women, hence the trade surname, 'brewster'. In a society where sugar was extremely expensive and honey scarce, thick ale was an important component of people's diet. But the sugar had fermented in the best ale. Originally ale would be fermented mash as is African beer today. Early British ales were made from successive extracts of a single batch of brown malt. The strongest batch produced the best quality 'strong' ale, the third extract the poorest 'small beer'.

Originally 'beer' meant hopped ale. Hops had been cultivated for beer brewing in the Low Countries since at least the beginning of the fourteenth century. They gave aroma and increased the bitterness, to offset the natural sweetness of ale. Most importantly to the publican, they improved the keeping quality of the brew. Broom, bayberries, and ivy-berries were also often used in brewing, but at some point hops became the only legal additive. Hops were probably introduced into English brewing by Flemings in about 1400. Then Flemings came themselves, settled and cultivated hops in Kent. By the mid sixteenth century the countryside around Maidstone was already called the Mother of Hop Grounds. A popular jingle dates the advent of hops more precisely:

'Hops, Reformation, bays and beer,
Came to England all in a year.'

Maidstone was overtaken by Canterbury where, by the early eighteenth century Defoe reported no fewer than 6,000 acres devoted to hops. Little over half a century ago 40,000 East Londoners would travel annually to the hopfields of Kent for the three-week harvest period. The work was poorly paid, but it was a break in the countryside from the slums of the East End.

The terms 'beer' and 'ale' in due course became synonymous but the introduction of hops aroused strong feelings. By the second half of the seventeenth century hops were firmly established but still viewed by some as interlopers, perhaps because immigrants had introduced their cultivation. John Evelyn referred in his diary to hops as 'that noxious weed.' Over a century earlier, when hop cultivation in England was still relatively new, one patriotic physician wrote in 1542:

'Ale is made of malte and water... Ale for an Englysche man is a naturall drinke. ... Barly malte maketh better ale than oten

malte or any other corne doth. It doth engendre grose
humoures but yette it maketh a man strong….

Bere is made of malte, of hoppes, and water; it is the
naturall drynke for a Dutche man, and nowe of lete dayes it
is much used in England to the detryment of many Englysshe
people... It doth make a man fat, and doth inflate the bely, as
it doth appere by the Dutche men's faces and belyes.'

So, now you know. When next you see a football fan waving the
flag of St George, don't look at the flag but at his gut. Then you'll
know if he is in fact acting under unpatriotic and alien influences.

By the seventeenth century, if not earlier, small beer had become
the standard household drink, cheap, of low alcohol and much
safer than water. It was taken at meals and between meals. It was
consumed in vast quantities. The increasing demand led to the
decline of the domestic brewers and the establishment of 'common'
breweries, forerunners of today's large breweries. In the mid-
eighteenth century Benjamin Franklin described daily beer-drinking
in a London printing-house: men took a pint before breakfast, a pint
with breakfast, a pint at midday dinner, a pint at six and a pint when
work was 'knocked off'. And those three quarts were consumed
before any evening drinking might begin. There were, at that time,
3,200 alehouses, besides over 7,000 gin shops feeding London's
alcoholic thirst.

It was in the eighteenth century that London brewers perfected a
popular new mellow drink, porter, with a strong dark colour, sweet
and highly hopped. It acquired its name because of its particular
popularity with the porter population of the great London markets.
Porter is the forerunner of 'stout', a drink developed in London
before being adopted elsewhere. The eighteenth century growth of
beer consumption led to an increase in tax on malt. As a result
brewers added more hops and less malt to their brew. It was the

increase in hops which created 'bitter': too bitter for many then and still too bitter for some. Drinkers often mixed bitter with porter or stout, calling it 'half-and-half'.

It is only in the last 30 years that lager type beer has gained its ascendancy in the UK. Few brewers in the UK have had the confidence to establish their own brands of lager and many brew here under licence from the original brewers in Europe, the US or Australia.

The last word on ale must go to John Taylor (1580-1663). Taylor, known for his boisterous prose and poetry, ended his days as a publican in Long Acre. Before then he had been a London waterman and been pressed into the navy. Aged almost 40 and certainly old enough to know better, he set out from London for the Isle of Sheppey in a brown paper boat and narrowly escaped drowning. What a clot, but one cannot fault his paean to ale:

> 'It is called Merry-go-down for it slides down merrily; It is fragrant to the scent; It is most pleasing to the taste.... It is Touching or Feeling to the Brain and Heart; and (to please the senses all) it provokes me to singing and mirth..... The speedy taking of it doth comfort a heavy and troubled mind; it will make a weeping widow laugh and forget sorrow for her dead husband.... It will set a Bashful suitor a–wooing. It heats the blood of the Aged; It will cause a man to speak past his own or any other mans capacity or understanding; It sets an edge upon Logic and Rhetoric; It is a friend to the Muses.... It puts eloquence into the Orator; It will make the Philosopher talk profoundly, the Scholar learnedly, and the Lawyer Acute and feelingly.... It is a great friend to Truth, for they that drink of it will reveal all they know, be it never so secret to be kept... It will put Courage into a Coward and make him swagger and fight; It is a seal to many a good Bargain. The Physician will commend it; the Lawyer will

defend it. It neither hurts nor kills any but those that abuse it unmeasurably and beyond bearing; it doth good to as many as take it rightly... And in conclusion it is such a nourisher of Mankind, that if my mouth were as big as Bishopsgate, my Pen as long as a Maypole, and my Ink a flowing spring, or a standing fishpond, yet I could not with Mouth, Pen, or Inke, speak or write the true worth and worthwhileness of Ale.'

And so it is time for a drink.

Index